RELEASE ME

RELEASE ME

Vicky Harrison

Library of Congress Control Number:		2016910388
ISBN:	Hardcover	978-1-5245-1261-3
	Softcover	978-1-5245-1260-6
	eBook	978-1-5245-1259-0

Print information available on the last page.

Rev. date: 09/12/2016

To order additional copies of this book, contact:
Xlibris
1-888-795-4274
www.Xlibris.com
Orders@Xlibris.com
739893

CONTENTS

DEDICATION PAGE

To my first born child, Tyler,

I love you in this life and in all the lives to come. You are a beautiful soul who got twisted along the way. You taught me more than I ever knew that I could learn about life and love.

To Ron and Seth,

You are my rocks. You have helped hold me together. You put up with more than any father and brother should or most would. You are both so strong. I love you both deeply.

To my friends and family,

I honestly don't know where or who I would be without your undying support. Thanks for listening, for allowing me to cry on your shoulders, and for your constant love.

January 2002 (8th Grade)

Dear Tyler,

Thanks for being open with me and trusting me enough to sit down with me last Saturday afternoon, and tell me how depressed you are. I honestly had no idea. It was obvious from your words, as well as your body language (I won't tell you how you had snot running down your face as you were sobbing), that you are very, very depressed and upset. (I won't also tell you how sad, disappointed, and ignorant I feel right now. For goodness sake! I have a Masters Degree in education, and work with kids all day long! It generally doesn't take a rocket scientist to see if kids are depressed. How could I not have seen this in my firstborn son? One of three people that I love more than anyone else in the world? No signs at all? Clearly, you blew me away last weekend. I truly thought I was much more in tune to you . . . I thought I was perceptive, astute, halfway smart, a decent Mom). I promise you that we will talk often. I will support you and we will do what we need to do as a family. I will get you the best counselor to talk to that I can find. I will help you get medication if you need it, and you will feel better.

Love,
Moo

Dear Moo (paraphrased by Tyler's mom),

You have no idea how miserable I am. I am lonely. I am alone. I feel as though no one really gets me. You try, but I'm different from everyone else in our family, in our neighborhood, and in my class.

When I feel, it goes so deep. Right now, I am so sad and it is permeating my every pore, cell, thought, and feeling. I don't even know why I am sad. When I write poetry and draw, it makes me feel somewhat better, but knowing that if someone would read it and still wouldn't get me or truly comprehend and understand what I'm saying, it would make me feel even worse.

Why am I like this? Why do I care so much about things that no one else does? Why am I so lonely even though I have lots of friends? Why am I the only one like this? Even in my own house? None of you draw, write, or seem burdened by daily life. Dad is always cleaning and you're cooking; Seth is a pain, being nine years old. It is very lonely in the place that I love most—my home, my room . . .

Love,
Tyler

SPRING 2002
(8ᵀᴴ GRADE)

CERTIFICATE OF ACHIEVEMENT

May it be known that

TYLER HARRISON

has completed the curriculum in
Drug Abuse Resistance Education (D.A.R.E.) and has
made a personal commitment to avoid the pressures to
begin using drugs.

Douglas L. Knight, President
Ohio Association of Chiefs of Police

Betty D. Montgomery
Attorney General

John M. Goff
Superintendent of Public Instruction
Ohio Department of Education

Rolando M. Newton

D.A.R.E. Officer

Printed on Recycled Paper

Spring 2002
(8th Grade)

Dear Tyler,

I sure hope you are feeling better now that you are seeing a therapist. I feel somewhat relieved, I must say. Knowing what the childhood developmental stages are for kids of all ages including teenagers, it is really difficult for me to ascertain the difference between true angst on your part and what is typical for boys/kids your age. I love you so much and care about you at such a deep level; all I ever want for you and Seth to be healthy and happy. I will do whatever I know how to do to make that happen. I know that I cannot be objective, and I believe in the power of counseling, so hopefully this will help you.

Love,
Moo

Dear Tyler,

I am so glad that you are seeing a counselor. I totally get doctor-patient confidentiality, HIPA rules, etc., but I wish that the doctor would give me a little bit more feedback about what could be the root of your problem. I really have no idea why why you are depressed. Sure, Dad and I fight sometimes, and I know that you don't have as many nice things as some as the kids you go to school with, but other than that, I cannot figure out why you are depressed. Of course, I know that sometimes people just get depressed for no reason, and that there are a variety of depression classifications in the DSM-IV, but I just can't wrap my head around why you were so very upset. You've always been so articulate and open with me and you don't seem to know either why you're depressed. I love you so much and all I want is for you to be happy and healthy.

Love,
Moo

Dear Moo (paraphrased by Tyler's mom),

I don't fit in. The older I get, the less I fit. Other boys aren't like me. Other cool boys aren't interested in art class and all the things we do in there. The kids that I have hung out with since we moved to this neighborhood and to this school district since 3rd grade are playing school sports. I'm not good enough to be on any team. Sure, I'm on that roller hockey team in Westerville, where I don't know anyone and there's no one else from my school on that league. . . None of the guys at school know anything about roller hockey. I love doing ollies and kickflips on my skateboard, but my friends don't even have skateboards. What's wrong with me? And I don't seem to fit in with the other guys in this family either. Seth and Dad like the same sports like football and basketball, but I'm more interested in ice hockey and tennis. I just feel really lonely a lot of the time. I know that you want to help me, Mom, and the counseling is helping a little, but I have to figure this out on my own.

Love,
Tyler

MAY 2002
(END 8TH GRADE)

Dear Tyler,

I am so excited for you to go to Washington DC with the other 8th graders. It was a chunk of change to come up with (yes, money always seems to be tight), but it will be so worth it for you to see our nation's capital (something your dad and I have never done, but would love to see), and learn about the founding fathers of our country, government, and rich heritage. You will get to stay with your friends and do something really fun. I am hoping that this will be the turning point for you. You will see how many friends you have and perhaps, even come home with some new ones. I pray that since this trip precedes summer vacation, that after this trip and some fun times this summer, you will be back to your "old self".

Love,
Moo

Dear Tyler,

What do you mean you have no friends to room with in Washington DC? Are you kidding that you don't even want to go, after we paid all this money? How can you not have tons of kids to sit with on the bus? You're such a nice, cute boy, and all the other moms always tell me how polite and good you are. You have to be loved by your peers! I don't understand any of this. What is happening?

Love,
Moo

Dear Tyler,

Well, at least you found someone that you remotely like to sit with on the bus. I hope and pray that you will have fun.

Love,
Moo

OCTOBER 2002
(9ᵀᴴ GRADE)

Dear Tyler,

The summer didn't seem as fun for you as I'd hoped. I tried to come up with fun things to do that didn't cost a lot of money, but you didn't really seem very interested in anything. I was also sad that you didn't like your DC trip. It's not at all how I had envisioned or hoped that your experience would unfold. I sure hope you get involved in school activities, as I've suggested to you before, because there are so many things that your nationally renowned High School has to offer. I'm really at a loss to even suggest what you could get involved in because you only seem remotely interested in roller hockey, and there's no team at Scioto for that. I really want and need you to be connected within your school. I know how important that this year in High School is and so hope will be a better experience for you than the last year or so. Please, Tyler, I need for this to be a good year for you. I know how pivotal this year can be in your life.

Love,
Moo

Dear Tyler,

I am so glad that you decided to play ice hockey for the high school's team. It's a brand new sport for the school, so you will get in on the ground floor and be part of something good and positive. Hopefully you will make some new, decent friends and this will be a great experience for you. The roller hockey that you played recently didn't help you make any friends since it wasn't local. I know that you're not interested in many sports that other boys are, such as basketball or football, so I'm thrilled that you will play ice hockey. It's really expensive but we will make it work. We will go to Play it Again Sports and get you some used equipment and it will be fun. I am excited to watch you play. You have always loved skating, whether it's on roller blades, your skateboard, roller hockey, or ice hockey and you're pretty good at it, so I bet you will play a lot.

Love,
Moo

Dear Tyler,

What happened to all of your guy friends? I keep hearing about Liz, and you keep bringing over all of these girls that I never heard of, since they went to different elementary and middle schools. Where did you meet these girls if they're not in your classes? Why aren't you hanging out with any guys? Surely they're not all playing football or basketball after school. I don't understand you, Tyler. Thank God you are playing hockey! You need to keep busy.

Love,
Moo

OCTOBER 2002 (9TH GRADE)

Dear Tyler,

I don't even know how to express the realization that I came to at curriculum night at your high school. When your art teacher told your dad and I that you were talented, we politely agreed and said that you had been drawing since you were three years old. But, when she showed us a picture of your work and then showed us a completed project of an average student's, it was so obvious just how skilled and talented that you are. I always knew that you had talent, but since I'm not an artist and don't really know much about it, I had no idea just how talented you really are. I'm so proud of you. You will go far in life. You will accomplish so much with that talent of yours. I cannot wait to see who you will become and what you decide to do vocationally. There are so many opportunities waiting for you. It's so exciting! I'm just so impressed by and proud of you.

Love,
Moo

Dear Tyler,

I'm so glad that you're working at Kroger's and that you are operating the cash register! You worked your way up from gathering carts to the register and I'm so proud of you. The money is really helpful, as now you are earning your spending money. I'm also relieved to know where you are and what you are doing for fifteen hours of the week! My friends say that they like to talk to talk to you when they grocery shop because you are always so polite and friendly. I am so proud of you. I love you so much.

Love,
Moo

FEBRUARY 2003 (9TH GRADE)

Dear Tyler,

I know that you are not playing as much hockey as you'd hoped, but I'm glad that you play some, and that you made a goal tonight in the game! I get so cold watching you play with my Raynaud's Syndrome, but it is so worth it because you are part of a team, part of a school group. You seem happy and there doesn't seem to be any negatives. This is a good year and I'm so glad. You needed this positive year. I have great hope for the remainder of your high school years now. I feel truly optimistic for the first time in a while. You have so much talent and your teachers recognize it. You will go far in life. I just know it.

Love,
Moo

APRIL 2003
(9ᵀᴴ GRADE)

Third Quarter Report Card

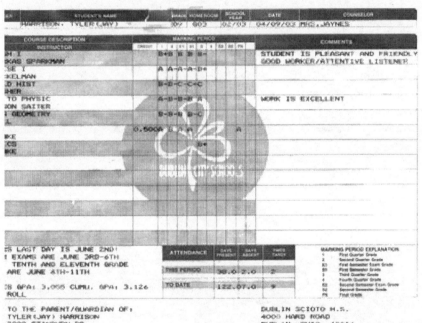

OCTOBER 2003 (10TH GRADE)

Dear Tyler,

Are you sure you don't want to play ice hockey? Why not? What do you mean? The coach called you personally to ask you why you didn't want to play, and he tried to talk you into rejoining the team. Are you positive you don't want to? You need to be involved with something. What are you going to do if you don't play hockey? I realize that you have a job now, but you need to be involved with something at your school, in order for you to connect and feel as though you belong. It's so hard for me to understand, as I loved being involved in many activities while in H.S. You're good with computers, a great photographer, great in all aspects of art, and you enjoyed playing ice hockey. . .I just don't understand why you don't want to be a part of a group and have a group of friends who are interested in the same things that you're interested in and good at. Please help me understand you, Tyler. I really want to know what is happening.

Love,
Moo

NOVEMBER 2003 (10ᵀᴴ GRADE)

First Quarter Report Card

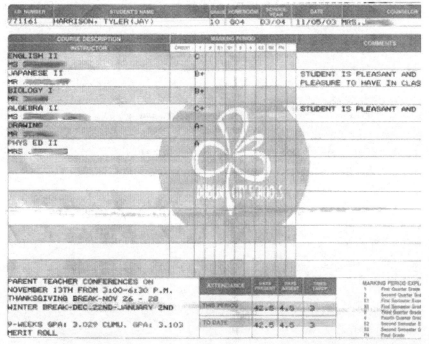

ID NUMBER	STUDENT'S NAME	GRADE	HOMEROOM	SCHOOL YEAR	DATE	COUNSELOR
771161	HARRISON, TYLER(JAY)	10	904	03/04	11/05/03	MRS. ⬛

COURSE DESCRIPTION / INSTRUCTOR	CREDIT	MARKING PERIOD	COMMENTS
ENGLISH II / MS ⬛	C		
JAPANESE II / MR ⬛	B+		STUDENT IS PLEASANT AND PLEASURE TO HAVE IN CLAS
BIOLOGY I / MR ⬛	B+		
ALGEBRA II / MS ⬛	C+		STUDENT IS PLEASANT AND
DRAWING / MR ⬛	A-		
PHYS ED II / MRS ⬛	A		

PARENT TEACHER CONFERENCES ON
NOVEMBER 13TH FROM 3:00-6:30 P.M.
THANKSGIVING BREAK-NOV 26 - 28
WINTER BREAK-DEC.22ND-JANUARY 2ND

9-WEEKS GPA: 3.029 CUMU. GPA: 3.103
MERIT ROLL

ATTENDANCE	DAYS PRESENT	DAYS ABSENT	TIMES TARDY
THIS PERIOD	42.5	4.5	3
TO DATE	42.5	4.5	3

MARKING PERIOD EXPL.
1 First Quarter Grade
2 Second Quarter Gr
3 First Semester Exam
1S First Semester Grad
3 Third Quarter Grade
4 Fourth Quarter Grad
2 Second Semester E
2S Second Semester G
FN Final Grade

TO THE PARENT/GUARDIAN OF:
TYLER(JAY) HARRISON
7929 STANBURN RD
DUBLIN, OH 43016

DUBLIN SCIOTO H.S.
4000 HARD ROAD
DUBLIN, OHIO 43016
MS. MARINA DAVIS, PRINCI

*GRADING INFORMATION ON REVERSE SIDE

July 2004
(Before 11th Grade)

Tyler,

I am sooooooooo freaking mad at you right now! I don't even know where to begin. First of all, I NEVER get a pedicure and I decided after the parade that I would splurge and get a $35 pedicure at one of those walk-in places before they close. Here I am, trying to savor every second of this rare indulgence, and Seth starts blowing up my phone, telling me that you're smoking pot. IN OUR HOUSE. He's scared to death. Seriously, you are smoking pot? Where did you get that crap? And remember, your brother is young! I can't have him exposed to that shit. He doesn't even know what it is. He just smelled something really bad and was worried the house would burn down. Where the hell is your dad and why doesn't he ever answer his phone? Why do you do such stupid stuff? You cause me a lot of stress. This is supposed to be a happy, fun holiday, Tyler!

In frustration,
Moo

JULY 2004
(BEFORE 11ᵀᴴ GRADE)

Dear Seth,

You are doing the right thing by telling me what Tyler is doing. I'm so glad that you called me to say that you smelled smoke, and tell me you thought Tyler was smoking pot. You need to always tell me what you see, hear, smell, whatever. You know that drugs are very bad for you. Tyler made a mistake by smoking that marijuana that someone gave to him. He was experimenting in our house and he shouldn't have. Sometimes, that's what teenagers do. But experimenting with drugs is very dangerous and he shouldn't have done that. I'm sorry you were scared. Just remember to always tell me when it happens, okay? I love you, Doody Bug.

Love,
Mom

AUGUST 2004 (BEFORE 11ᵀᴴ GRADE)

Dear Tyler,

WTH? What is this crap that I just happened to "find" (yes, I realize that you know that Seth is narcing on you) in your desk? You're growing weed in your freaking desk? Is that what this is? Are you kidding me? THIS is what you use your desk for? What are all these lights rigged into the desk? How did you know how to do this? What are you going to do with all of these weed? Are you going to smoke or sell it? What am I going to do with you? I hope that this new counselor can help you, and me also because you need to get serious about straightening up your life. This is not how you were raised. Your dad and I have never done drugs, and while we both had some wild streaks in our late teen years, we never did anything like this. I don't want to see you throw your life away by making some stupid mistakes. Please remember also that you are a role model for your four year younger brother! It's bad enough that you would smoke weed. But in our house? And be growing it in your desk? Who does that?

In disbelief,
Moo

AUGUST 2004
(BEFORE 11ᵀᴴ GRADE)

Dear Tyler,

What happened last night? OMG!. Your dad and I were frightened and in shock. We, being in bed and asleep, heard a loud noise coming from downstairs. You were down in the basement and then in our family room, out of control. It's like we saw you and yet, it wasn't you because you were flailing around, acting all wild, jumping on furniture, etc. Then, we talked to your good friend and she said that you took a drug called 2CB. I was so scared until the paramedics got to our house and transported you to Riverside Hospital. I'm glad that I stayed beside you all the way and was there with you in the hospital when they gave you charcoal, and your vitals began improving. What is 2CB? Where did you get it? Why did you take it? What were you thinking? Please talk to me, Tyler. We have always been so close. You have always shared your deepest feelings with me. Why are you taking drugs? I know that you're smart enough to know the possible consequences. Why would you do this? Are you sad? Mad? Upset? Curious? What can I do to help you? I sure hope that this new counselor can you help you. And I hope she can help me too. . .

Feeling scared,
Moo

October 2004 (11th Grade)

"Hello? This is Tyler's friend, Xyz? I don't understand what you are telling me. You are saying that Tyler is using cocaine? Are you sure? I am just so shocked. I had no idea. You are positive? Thanks for telling me. No, I won't tell Tyler who told me."

OCTOBER 2004
(11ᵀᴴ GRADE)

Dear Tyler,

I just don't understand what is happening. We took you to that drug testing place to determine whether or not you are using cocaine, and when they say that you are, you provide all of this research for us about false positives. I told you that I ran into a parent in the grocery store who told me that their son said that you are using cocaine; that's how I was informed. No, I'm not going to say who it was. If this drug place says that you are using cocaine and someone saw you use it, you must be using it. We have to get you some help. Why do you say that you're not using any drugs? Yes, you made the point that you are still getting really good grades, but you have lost weight and you seem a little bit hyper. I don't know what to do, Tyler. You have to be honest with me in order for me to help you. What is going on with you? I am at wit's end with you!

Trying to frantically understand,
Moo

October 2004
(11th Grade)

Today I messed up. I messed up real bad. It wasn't the worst thing I've done, but now I know. I know that I am smart. I know what the things that I should cherish are, not the things that I pay attention to. What do I mean? I mean I hugged my father today for the first time since I can even remember. I love my family. If I had to decide who had to die right now... if I was told it was either me or my mom, I'd go. If it was me or my dad, I'd go. If it was me or Seth, I'd go. My life is completely out of perspective. My grades are not good, my family does not trust me, and my biggest fear of all is that they no longer love me. Believe it or not, I got it all straightened out today. I know it will be hard for my family to forgive me. But I am going to try my best. I love them. I never want to hurt any of them again. You know why I would never be able to commit suicide? It's not because of my friends. I'm not afraid to do it. But it really is my family. When my mother asks me to play cards and I blow her off I feel terrible. When my father won't look into my eyes I want to die. And when my brother tells me I failed him. I wish I was never born. It makes me feel bad when my mother tells me she's proud of me. I love it when dad puts his ego to the side and tells me I did a good job I love both of my parents. They are two of the most amazing people I have ever met.

I DONT WANT
TO FEEL LIKE
THIS ANYMORE

I want to make it right, mom I love you. These are the words coming straight from my heart, to my fingers to put it into writing. You are both wonderful parents. The proof is my life. If you were bad parents, or if I didn't really love you, I would be dead. My one regret is not telling my parents everything I didn't tell you when I made a new friend, I never told you that I loved you. detail about my day, I never told you that I loved you and of course this made it a lot harder to talk about serious things with you guys, and it's my fault 100%.

This is how much I love you mom:
- I love it when I get to see you smile
- I come to you first when I have a problem
- I have not harmed myself because I imagine you being proud of me many years from now.

I want to make it up to you, mom I love you. I really do. and I PROMISE I will make you proud to be my mother, and when I am at that point, I'm going to tell everyone how it was you, I'll tell them my mom molded me into the person that I am. I'm not asking you to trust me. I just want to know that both you and dad still love me. And in 10 years or so, you'll see how proud I can make you. Thanks for reading, I wrote it all as it came to me in my head. So it only took 30 minutes or so to write, but I cried the entire time. I don't ever want to let you down.

Love always (Please),

Tyler

OCTOBER 2004
(11ᵀᴴ GRADE)

Dear Tyler,

I am so happy that you want to be a camp counselor for the 8th graders, Tyler, because you've always loved kids and are great with them. What a wonderful opportunity for you to be a leader! Someone that younger kids can look up to. I know that you will be good with the kids and make it fun for them. I have to say, though, that I'm a little bit worried with all the drug issues. God, Tyler, please don't take drugs to camp. Don't let little kids see you do drugs. You wouldn't do that, would you? You talk about wanting to be an art teacher. Here's a chance to be around younger kids over an extended period of time. Please be a good role model!

Love,
Moo

8218 ~~~~~~
Dublin, Ohio 43016
October 28, 2004

Dear Tyler (AKA Axel),

Hi I was a your cabin for Outdoor ED. I'm
going to tell you my nickname and you figure out what
my real name is. It is ~~~~~ or however you spell it.
I'll tell what my name is at the end. I just wanted to
say I had a good time when I was around you expecily
playing football and I knock you over hahaha also when
you attacked me as an owl and knock out about th skins
and only left two while I got my head stuck in a jar.
It was fun ~~having~~ nicknames that you gave all of us.
It was pretty much fun being around you, it was
even better when all of team Bacon was there.

 Love,

2490
Dublin, Ohio 43016

Dear Tyler,

I had a great time at camp. This is _____ or a.k.a. Sparky in your cabin. My favorite thing about was getting to know new people. and when you let us interact with other cabins. You let us do fun things in the cabin when we were bored. It was funny when we gave you the a.k.a. Fartknocher and when we named our cabin team bacon. I hope that we will meet again in the future so we can be buddies.

Sincerely,

November 2004
(11ᵀᴴ Grade)

Dear Tyler,

What a crazy puppy you picked. I love the name, Vinnie! I am sad also that we had to put our other dog down, Elvis, but Vinnie is adorable. He's a stinker and is so ornery. He's always getting into things but I can tell that he really loves you and I think he's going to primarily be your dog. Elvis was always following me around, but I bet Vinnie will love you the most.

I am hoping that this crazy pet of yours will be the distraction that you need to think about positive connections, love, and family, as well as being a nurturing caretaker, which seems to come so easily and natural to you. Let these positives overtake any thoughts of negative things such as smoking pot or using 2 CB or any other drugs. I'm counting on your focusing on the positives, Tyler . . .

I love the artwork that you are producing in your classes. You are obviously very talented. I cannot wait to see what you do with all of that talent and skill after college! The world is your oyster!

Love,
Moo

Tyler wrote this letter before starting the Talbot Hall Program (11-10-2004)

Tyler, dropping this us. Right before he started at Talbot Hall. (See note he signed. 11/10/04)

Dear Vicky,

I give you whatever you want to hear. I see you caught one of the baits I left. You must suck at searching my room, there are 3 more little letters I left for you to find. Do you really think I'd leave that right on top of my desk DATED and SIGNED? hahaha! You can think what you want to think, and since I obviously won't be shining the light of truth onto you, I'll help you out. Maybe next time I'll leave a razor on a big mirror and just let it sit on the kitchen counter. The point is, you're ignorant. Try and look at the real evidence here. I'll list it all below and explain it after.

Evidence for me	Evidence against me
• no paraphernalia anywhere in my possession	• drug test
• no depletion of funds necessary to support such a habit.	
• no friends calling you to tell you about my "problem"	
• no bloody noses	
• haven't gone anywhere any weekend in the past few weeks.	
• I sleep a lot	
• I eat	
• I am not aggressive	
• why would I lie knowing I would fail the test?	

we will start with the evidence against me 2
Drug tests that I "failed". Did you not listen to
a word I said when I came clean about the DXM
issue? Did you not see it on the internet? I showed
you a page saying that Dextromethorphan and
amoxicillin give off metabolites with matching
chemical compositions of the metabolites that
cocaine and other amphetamines give off when they
are broken down inside your body which, if you
knew anything, you'd know they test for the
metabolites, not the cocaine itself, because
the drug itself doesn't stay in your system, it
gets broken down. Call up Dr ██████, get online,
or read a book, buy yourself a big fat chemistry
book and read about the metabolites of amoxicillin
and cocaine, and Dextromethorphan and cocaine.
They are identical. Do your homework, I did mine.
If we took this as a case to trial I would
represent myself and the jury would find insufficient
evidence that I used cocaine. But I'm getting off
topic. Do your homework, read about what actually
happens in a cocaine drug test. Than consider the above.
So for now I consider the fact that I failed the drug tests
completely obsolete in regards to your case.
    Next we have a big list of things that will
be used in my defense. First up is no paraphernelia
needed to be a cocaine user is in my posession.
period. What do they need? Razors, glass plates
or big mirrors, straws, and little baggies with white
powder residue left inside. Have you found any of
that in my car? In my room? I don't think so. I even
offered to go out with you tuesday night to search
my car and room. You failed to take that opportunity.

Next item up for bids - Money. Let's see. I got a $100 paycheck almost TWO weeks ago right? I got $20 allowance almost one week ago you know I took ▓▓▓▓▓ out to BF changs, there goes $25. I'm down to $95, I also put $15 in for gas the day I cashed my check, down to $80. I bought Shrek 2 on DVD yesterday, to watch with ▓▓▓▓▓ Down to $60. Do we agree on all of this? If not, too bad, it's the truth. NOT to mention I got breakfast at McDonalds twice in this time and lunch from McDonalds once. Dad even saw me eating it. So really I should have about $50. I have $65. what is the point of all this? once again, if you would do your homework, you would know that in order to pass a cocaine drug test, you have to have stopped using it for a minimum of 2 days and a maximum of 4 days, sometimes longer if you're a chronic user. so that means that since I took the last test on wed. I would have had to use cocaine on saturday, at the very earliest in order to fail. which means I would have had to actually BUY the cocaine. so if that is the case, where did the money come from? Do your homework, one GRAM of cocaine costs about $50 on the street. That would mean I'd have little or no money right now, and that is just one gram. A gram weighs about the same as a paperclip. one gram of cocaine isn't worth a dealer to sell. selling a gram of cocaine to someone would be like you calling the Kelloggs cereal company and saying "I want 3 pieces of frosted mini wheats." They won't do it for you. End of story. I have $65 right now. Proof that I couldn't have bought cocaine and used it in

the allotted period of time that i had to still fail
a cocaine drug test on wednesday, let alone
saturday (the day of the first test) I hope you are
starting to see the truth.

Has ~~████████████~~
called you to tell you about me? No. The person
most likely to though is (to your probable surprise)
~~████~~. She dated a kid named ~~████████~~ He
snorted cocaine, a lot. He had big problems, he was
depressed, he cut himself, and he had no money
and no friends because of his problems He and ~~████~~
broke up and she hates him she calls him a useless
coke head. She hates the drug, she would never, ever
let me do it and if i did, she would tell you.
And you might be saying, "well maybe she doesn't
know." But how close are ~~███~~ and I? you know
we are very close, i simply wouldn't be able to
hide it from her. Call her up, ~~█████████~~ is her cell.
Ask her on the spot so she won't have time to lie
whatever it takes.

If you would research about the topic a little
bit, you'd read that people who do cocaine don't
eat regularly, don't sleep regularly, become very
aggressive physically, and tend to get bloody noses.
i go to bed at 10pm at the very latest. I eat
regularly, i haven't ever in my life gotten a bloody
nose, and i haven't been physically aggressive with
anyone. Don't you look like a fool now?

Next, do you remember what i spent last
weekend doing? sitting at home. Do you remember
what i did the weekend before that? i sat at
home. So my next question is... where am i doing
cocaine at? The effects of cocaine are creating

a state of euphoria and a huge burst of energy. So why would I want to be hyper sitting alone in the basement watching a movie? It doesn't make sense, Vicky. If I were on cocaine I'd be out at parties doing it and coming home late at night, unable to sleep. Hmmmm... maybe Tyler is telling the truth.

Last and certainly not least is the fact that you dragged me out of BW3* on Tuesday to tell me I had cocaine on a drug test. If I had done cocaine, why would I willingly subject and encourage you to get me screened asap? and why would I be so confident about the results. If you're laughing and saying "you did fail" you obviously didn't read the first paragraph of this paper. Does it make sense to you that a kid as smart as me would throw myself into the lion's den? That is stupid.

Now I'll move on to my closing statement. After reading this paper, how do you feel? It's 9:21 on Saturday the 13th and I am in the prison of CI or DSHS. I wrote this all in here. Now ask yourself if it is possible that I'm telling you the truth. If this was a court and you were a juror and my neck was on the line, and I laid all this shit on the table for you to soak up, would you write "guilty" on your silent ballot in the jury deciding room? I do not, have not, and will not use(d) cocaine. End of story, case closed.

So Vicky, what did you think of my defense? Pretty good, huh? An honest man has nothing to fear, and I am not afraid. If you are blissfully ignorant enough to still fully believe I use(d) cocaine, and you try to send me to rehab or anything like that, you will not see me breathing again. If you try to send me off, I will kill myself. And I am not joking. Don't fuck with me, I'll do it. And if you show this or mention this to anyone, you better hope I don't find out about it. I would rather take my own life than go down in history as a drug addict. What do you think of your son now Vicky? Are you going to show this to the police? Dr. ⬛⬛? Maybe dad? Best hope I don't find out about it. Because if I take my life, you are 100% responsible. Can you really live the rest of your life knowing that you're responsible for that? I don't think so.

Sincerely,
Prisoner # 101587

P.S. you brought this
on yourself.
Have a nice day
☺

DECEMBER 2004 (11ᵀᴴ GRADE)

Dear Tyler,

I am so glad that you/we're doing outpatient therapy at Talbot Hall at OSU. This program came highly recommended from your psychologist (it's helped me to see her too), as well as Doc Joe (a medical doctor who attended our former church; he specializes in drug addiction). I am optimistic that you can get the help that you need here and that we can also, as a family. I'm glad that they have a family group component, so that the three of us can also participate and hopefully learn what is going on and how we can support you. Nothing is more important than your health, Tyler.

You seem to be very open and willing to participate in this program. Does that mean you will learn lessons from what you did in the past and never do drugs again? I sure hope so, Tyler. I am so worried about you, but I do feel more confident that you will be on the right, good path now.

I hate it that you got fired at the café job! What happened? I thought you really liked that job and were doing well. I hope you didn't do anything terrible, as I got you that job through my friend at work. With his brother owning the place, I sure hope you didn't steal or anything! I will be so humiliated if you did. It was bad enough that you got fired from Kroger's because of pranks that you and ███ pulled on each other. I'm still not sure of exactly what happened at the store because you aren't saying much and neither is Kroger's, but this café job came through a friend, so it makes me nervous to recommend you again to anyone in the future that I know. Why would you do anything to get fired? You're a good worker, you're smart, you're personable, you have all of these positive traits. Are you impulsive? Are you on time? Do you do things before you think at work also? What is happening? I so want to understand, Tyler. I feel as though I cannot really help you unless I know exactly what is happening.

Trying to be hopeful,
Moo

JANUARY 2005
(11ᵀᴴ GRADE)

Dear Tyler,

Congratulations on being released from Talbot Hall's Adolescent Intensive Outpatient Program. The therapist indicated that you were actively engaged in group discussions, as well as treatment assignments. He said that your prognosis for the future is good. He recommended that you attend the AfterCare program at Talbot Hall but knows that you will likely go back to Doc Joe for regular drug screens, as well as 12-Step meetings instead.

I learned a lot from participating in those groups. When I see you amongst your peers in a group like that, it makes me realize how bright, talented, articulate, polite, and personable you are. Some of those kids have had very tough home lives, attitude issues, and were rude. You do not have those things in common with them whatsoever. I know that you also see the differences between you and many of them. You provided comments that showed how insightful and bright that you are. You were engaged, and you indicated multiple times that you want to stop using drugs. Many of the others did not.

I sure hope and pray that you will not start using drugs again, Tyler. This is a pivotal year. You need to be getting ready for college. You have to keep your grades up and do your best academically, emotionally, and physically. I know that you can do it, Tyler. I believe in you.

Optimistic and yet a little anxious,
Moo

FEBRUARY 2005 (11ᵀᴴ GRADE)

Dear Tyler,

You've had some good random drug screens at Doc Joe's since completing your outpatient treatment. Keep up the great work, Tyler. I'm optimistic that you are on the right track. I think you just went through a wild streak but now that you've done outpatient treatment and met some other kids and can see where they've been and where you could be headed if you keep using, I think you will stay on a more straight and narrow path. I pray to God you will, anyway. I love you so much, Tyler. I just want you to be healthy and happy.

Love,
Moo

March 1, 2005 (At DSHS during 11th Grade)

Tyler and another boy were found messing around in a restroom at school by a security officer. The other boy had a pink pill in his possession which Tyler said he knew nothing about. The other boy was also later found to have some bottles with prescribed Adderall, a medication for ADHD, and a straw. Tyler's backpack was examined and found to have sheets of printed counterfeit money in them. Prior to his car in the school parking lot being searched, and Tyler being asked what would be found, he admitted to having a bag of pot under the CD compartment. The officers found a Corona beer bottle converted into a marijuana pipe, as well as an empty vial and a Ziploc bag with urine in it.

Tyler wrote this at school before his parents arrived

Call for Service No._____
Case No. _05 7999_

WITNESS STATEMENT

I, _Tyler Harrison_____, am _17_ years old and I reside at
_7929 Stanburn Rd_____ in _Dublin_____, _Ohio_____,
and my phone number is _(614) 766-8084___. I hereby make the following statement
concerning _the counterfeit money in my backpack_____which
happened _~~at DSHS~~_____ on the _first_ day of _March_, ~~**~~ _2005_ at
aprox. 2:00 AM (PM)

    I am writing this witness statement to tell the truth, I
lied on one prior to this.

    My friend _____ and I coped the fronts of a
$20 bill and printed them, a lot. We did not cut them out,
did not ~~t_____~~ try to pass them anywhere. I do not think
_____ took ~~one~~ any of the bills but I am not sure. They were
found today.

      Tyler Harrison 3/1/05

    The $20 ~~a~~ that was photocoped was not a real $20, It
was a counterfeit that was found at my place of
employment, which is where I got the idea. I took the fake
$20 that my boss _____ found, and photocopied that, I then
burned it and threw the ashes away when I was done.

      Tyler Harrison 3/1/05

One L. Dull #55   _Tyler Harrison_   _3/1/05_

Signature of Officer   Signature of Witness   Date

FORM #2.2.HA3

POLICE

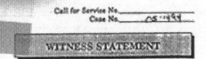

WITNESS STATEMENT

I, Tyler Harrison _____, am 17 years old and I reside at 7929 Stanburn Rd _____ in Dublin ~~⊘~~ _____ Ohio _____ and my phone number is (614) 766-8034 _____. I hereby make the following statement concerning Posession of marijuana + paraphenelia _____ which happened at Dublin Scioto HS ____ on the first day of March , ~~⊘~~ 2005 at appx 2:30 AM (PM)

_____

The pot that was found in my car was purchased from ~~_____~~ a student at scioto, we met in a parking lot and he gave it ~~to~~ to me, I had already paid him prior to receiving it. ~~I~~ ~~____~~ on friday of last week, I had met with him to give him my money, and he used my mini home made water pipe to get high. ~~_____~~ It was ~~____ _____~~ marijuana that was currently in my posession, I took one hit. we then put the piece under my ~~____~~ seat, and I took him home. ★ Bought 3.5g for $25.

Tyler Harrison 3/1/05

_____
_____
_____
_____
_____
_____
_____
_____
_____
_____
_____
_____
_____
_____
_____

Ofcr. R.P.M. #153   Tyler Harrison   3/1/05
Signature of Officer   Signature of Witness   Date

FORM 42.5.14A1

MARCH 4, 2005 (11ᵀᴴ GRADE)

Dear Tyler,

What are you doing? Why did you photocopy money? You are very smart, probably several IQ points beyond me (not that I believe I'm very smart; I do not) and you know that copying money is a federal crime. You could go to prison, Tyler! Were you planning on using that money? Really? You and your friend did that copying in my basement on my printer? Really? In our family's home? ? I am beyond stressed, words, and am in disbelief and shock. I am upset, worried, and frustrated. I don't know what to do with you. You are so cute and bright and unbelievably talented. Is this the route that you want to go in life? You are going to screw yourself royally. Not to mention us. Now, we will probably have to get an attorney. Does it look like we have money for an attorney? Does it look like we are able to take off and work and go to lawyer's offices and the courthouse? No and no! Come on Tyler, get with it. You have to get on the straight and narrow path! I am soooo worried about you.

Urine in your car? I know that I found empty bottles of urine in your room and accused you of using it to forge your drug tests at Doc Joe's, but I know that they come in the bathroom with you and watch you urinate, so how is carrying urine around helpful? It's gross and unsanitary, Tyler. You told me that you had it in your room because you had sleep issues and were so tired that you didn't want to get up and use the bathroom. I mostly believed you, but now that I find out that you have it in your car, I'm not so sure . . .

Pot in your car? At school? Why? Do you smoke it often? Daily? Are you addicted to it? Are you using other drugs as well? Were you trying to buy a stimulant from that other kid? Why? What is happening with you, Tyler?

In frustration,
Moo

MARCH 2005
(11ᵀᴴ GRADE)

Dear Tyler,

I just cannot believe what you told me. You've tried heroin and acid? You have been tested for HIV? Twice? You drove to Canada to get Everclear because it is 95% alcohol and you thought that was the only place to get it? You've been to crack houses? You've had a gun pointed at your head by a Coke dealer? Is this really true? OMG! OMG! I honestly have no idea what to do, say, or think. I want to help you, Tyler but I really don't know how. You have to be in an acute state for hospitals to admit you. You are not at that point, so I know that going to the ER, again, would be a waste of time. Rehabs out of state are soooo cost prohibitive. We do not begin to have the money to send you to any of those places. We are stretched to the max now. I've had you to so many counselors already, as well as to Doc Joe, several medical doctors, two private psychologists, and Talbot Hall. I don't know where to go next. God, I'm worried every second of every day about you. I feel as though I'm ignoring Seth because I'm so preoccupied with you. I feel as though I'm losing my mind . . .

At wit's end,
Moo

April 2005
(11th Grade)

(After 3-1, when DSNS police found pot in Tyler's car, I asked Tyler to write a contract in the use of his car, before it was allowed to drive again).

The Camry is not to be used to hold illegal substances, including cigarettes and paraphernelia.

The Camry is not to be used as a means to commit illegal actions such as delivering illegal substances or anything of that nature.

The Camry is not to be used in any way to help others commit illegal actions

The Camry is not to be used as an accessory to anything negative or illegal.

x [signature]

* By signing this contract you agree that you will abide by all above stated rules and that you do so by your own free will.

Not long after the signed contract, this picture was found in Tyler's room

4-8-05 (11th Grade)

Dear Mom,

I am sorry I got so out of control
over your computer and how I didn't
finish my job, I'm sorry I yelled
at you and was mean. I wish I
could take it all back already, because
you're my only mother and I love you
and I hate it when we're mad at
each other. Please forgive me.
on the flipside, I would appreciate it
if you got off my ass about getting
a job, I will pay my bills as soon
as I can but I am very obviously not
ready for a job right now. There is
just too much (although overlooked by
you) shit going on in my life and I
know that if I get a job and
am busy I will begin to use
drugs, and I know you don't want
that. I'm delaying getting a job
for my own personal health.

I'm sorry once again, please forgive
me, I'm very stressed out and
not a day goes by where I don't
feel like calling up ___ and buying
a nice bag of coke with money

that I don't even have, but I
don't because I know what it
would do to this family.

Love
Tyler

4-8-05 (11th Grade)

4/9/05   5:20 pm

I don't know anything. I feel like I am always fumbling around in the dark looking for something to hold onto. I keep finding sharp objects and I'm only hurting myself. I'm really scared my drug test is going to come up positive for pot on low levels considering ▮▮▮▮ hot boxed in my car on two different occasions the day before she went back to school... I won't know how to explain it to mom and dad... or ▮▮▮▮. I am completely fucked. I'm digging a hole into the pit of my heart and I keep getting handed bigger shovels.

I really tried to get my shit together at school but it was hard after being suspended. oh well, I'm sick of making excuses for why I am a complete failure... I fucked up. Plain and simple. I don't want to see mom cry... I don't want the test to come up positive. But I have a terrible feeling it's going to. Sometimes I just want to disappear and come back when I'm ready to. Once I get my shit together. It's hard. I want to suggest adderall to my parents but I know that won't go over well. I studied for my math quiz on adderall and I got a 42 out of 50 on it... 84% is pretty good I suppose.

I can never concentrate I'm always moving around I can't sit still. I'm getting fat. FUCK.

Why does everything suck? I am so thankful for ████. I would probably be too fucked up right now to write if it weren't for his help and support. I suppose things can always get worse right? That is no excuse as to why I am so messed up right now though. I have so much inside my head all at once I can't write fast enough to put it all down coherently.

I want to leave. I want to leave.

THIS FUCKING PLACE

4-9-05 (11th Grade)

I was just reading through
some writing I had. I want you
to read this.

                Love,
                  Tyler

(Tyler sent this to me through
his bedroom window as I
was sitting on the deck!)

APRIL 12, 2005
(11ᵀᴴ GRADE)

Tyler was observed snorting cocaine through a straw in one of his classes. He was in a separate room, sitting alone, when his parents got to the school. His mom and dad watched him get handcuffed and transported to a juvenile detention center for:

-possession of 2.15 grams of cocaine
-possession of <100 grams of marijuana
-possession of eighteen sheets of counterfeit US Currency

Winslor

(4-12-05) 4-12-05
(Tyler gave tom
when I got c
DSHS)

mom, first of all, I love you. I love you mom.
I'm so sorry. I know you have heard this
all before but I really really screwed up
this time. I love you mom, I don't want
to be like this anymore. I want to
change. I'll do anything it takes to
change. I love you mom, and I'm sorry.
I hate myself right now, as you probably do
too. I love you so much mom... I'm your son
and I just want you to know that I
really love you all and I want to
work this out. But the only thing I don't
want is you to hate me. I know you
won't trust me and I know you will
be mad but please don't hate me. Please
oh please all I want is for you to
love me and help me. I really do want
to change but it's just been so hard
and so rough... I am trying to be cooperative
and I want and need a hug from you.
If you don't want to give me one
though I understand if you do, I could
use one asap. I love you mom. You truly
are my hero. This is going to be hard mom,
this is going to be hard; but I'm glad
I got caught today. I had been thinking
and planning for a relapse for a while

now and I did it. I did. It was the dumbest
thing I have ever done so far. I should
have talked to you on sunday. God I
should have told you. It's hard for
me to express myself and I'm really sad
and upset about how things in my
life are and I just want to get better,
It's no reason to use, I know that,
It was stupid. I love you. I don't know
what else to say. I love you and the
rest of the family and I want to get
better. I'm sorry, please still love me.

Love, (please
Tyler

APRIL 12, 2005 (11ᵀᴴ GRADE)

Dear Tyler,

Oh, my God! Oh, my God! Oh, my God! Tyler, I am soooo scared. For you. For your life. For me. For our family. Financially. For your future life and career, and college, and everything. I am scared to death, Tyler. You are using cocaine again? You actually laid on the floor of your English class and snorted cocaine through a straw? I'm no Einstein, but it certainly seems as though you wanted to get caught to do something like that. Did you do it as a plea for help? What kind of help/attention did you hope to gain? I thought you were finished with cocaine? I thought this was behind us . . .

Oh, my God! You are in jail right now. You are not here with us. I just heard your dad sobbing. Seth will be devastated. Your dog misses you. I feel as though I can't get enough air to breathe. My heart rate has skyrocketed. I have to go outside to breathe. I feel as though my world has crashed. And yet everything looks the same. How can everything be so different and yet look the same? Nothing is the same. It will never be the same. I've been an educator for years and now my son was arrested at his school for snorting cocaine in his English class. My firstborn son, my baby, is in jail. Our family is devastated. Torn apart. Ripped up. Oh, my God.

When will I see you? What is the next step? Will you be okay? Will another kid harm you in juvie? You are not a juvie type of kid. You're a clean cut, smart, articulate, adorable kid who lives in a nice suburb of Columbus, in Dublin. You are from a good family. A middle class family. You were raised in church. You were an acolyte (lit the candles). You went through confirmation and have participated in the church's youth group. You played in the bell choir at church. You were always such a good little boy. What has happened to you? Are you still a good person? Do you know right from wrong? What is at your core? I cannot believe you would want this kind of life. Do you?

I still love you, Tyler. I will always love you, no matter what you do. I want to help you fix this. I want you to NEVER be involved with the law again. I want you to finish high school, finish college, and get into an art career that you love. I want you to see what all the world can be, and how fulfilling life is without any drug use or abuse. I want you to feel worthy and loved because you are. Do you feel worthy and loved, Tyler? I don't think that you do. Thanks for the note that you gave to me at school. How could you ever consider for one millisecond that I wouldn't or couldn't love you? I will always love you, even if you end up in prison for the rest of your life. You are my firstborn son. We are close. We take walks. I watch you do ollies on your skateboard at Olde Sawmill Elementary school. We play tennis. We walk Vinnie. You love Vinnie and he loves you. We play rummy and you win most of the time. I don't care that I don't win, because we are spending time together and talking. I am so connected to you mentally, emotionally, and spiritually. I always have been and I believe that I always will be. Tyler, please, turn your life around. If there's one hope, I am hoping that this situation will make you realize what the rest of your life could be if you don't straighten up. Oh, God, Tyler, what is happening there in juvie?

Love (forever),
Moo

Letter from Juvie

Dear Moo Moo and Tasha,   4/14/05

how's it going? It's getting better here in some terms and worse in others. I went to school today... science and english. We asked any question we wanted and I completely stumped him for fun. hehe. The day has gone by a little quicker, I read 104 pages in Harry Potter. We got to go outside today, it's nice out. I beat two kids in chess and I read Greek mythology to the class. I'm still in overflow but I was in a pod for a little just because 2 kids got sent to solitary confinement.

I found out the kid's name who called me gay. He is still bothering me... He's a "level 3" so he is allowed to go anywhere inside a pod, meaning they'll let him into my room while I'm sleeping. That really kind of scares me because he (   ) said he's going to come in, eat my ass and rape me. I don't really think he will, but he didn't sound like he was joking around. I requested to not be anywhere near him for those reasons. They didn't seem to care though. Not much else is going on. I'm back in the holding room with the rest of overflow right now, I believe it's sometime around 2pm. I ate a hot dog for lunch today. It wasn't so bad, it was the first thing we had the whole time in here aside from the pineapple I had on tuesday. Ah just in time!

he found me some paper. I'm probably
going to be level 1 very soon
so you might get a phone call
from me on friday, I'm really looking
forward to that.

How are things going at home? is
everything ok? I hope you guys are
able to maintain without me. I'm
kind of excited to be getting help soon
at fox run; amere said it's nice there.
I'll be a brand new man when I come back,
it's exciting.

I'm finally really realizing how much
I have and I feel bad for taking it all
for granted. I've got so many advantages
and I don't even take them, so many
opportunities that I'm not taking. It's
sad. I'm going to bust my ass when
I get out to get good grades and goto
to school and get a good job, be healthy
and happy. I'm sure you're crying and
smiling by now... I love you momma
and tasha. Tell seth I miss him too,
which I never thought I'd say. Tell
him he's not a "gangsta" though...
trust me. haha! alright well I'm
gonna go. I look forward to calling
you tomorrow. bye bye. xoxo

                        Love,
                        Tyler

April 18, 2005 (11ᵗʰ Grade)

Dear Tyler,

I am so happy that you are out of juvie, but now you must do some soul-searching and work to find out why you are using and what you need to do to stop. IF you <u>want</u> to stop, which I pray to God that you do. We are going to have you admitted to a psychiatric hospital after juvie and then you will go to an inpatient treatment center for drug abuse. I pray that this course of action, as suggested by the attorney that we've hired, will help you. I pray that you will learn what you need to learn so that you never make these mistakes again. I pray that you will be the person you used to be—a person who upholds his family's values, a person not interested in illegal activity A person who is not an addict. A person who wants to live life fully more than he wants to use illicit drugs.

We have your expulsion hearing for school on April 25, 2005. I pray to God that you can salvage this school year and graduate with your classmates. I have no idea what will happen. I am so worried, Tyler, but I am also relieved that we have a plan now. It seems like it takes something terrible to happen in order to get help, but at least, now we have a plan. A plan for rehab. A place that although it will be difficult to afford, we can make it happen. A place that's close enough that we can visit you each week, or however often visitation is allowed. Having a plan and a place for you to get help makes me feel a little bit better.

I love you, Tyler and I always want the best for you.

Love,
Moo

Letter from Doc Joe, Tyler's Drug Doctor who did monthly screens & consulting with Tyler

April 13, 2005

Dear Tyler:

I hope this note will remind you that I am thinking and praying for you daily.

I know you probably feel like the bottom of your world has fallen out, and in truth, it has. You have done some really stupid stuff. BUT, this is not the end of the book. You still have time to pull you life together and be the terrific person you were born to be.

Tyler, when we talked in my office, I asked you about your beliefs. Working your 12 steps, you have been taught to seek that higher power for help and guidance. Unfortunately, you gave up on the real Higher Power and went with your dead dog instead. From my perspective, that doesn't seem to be going too well for you. So, please indulge an old man and listen to a few words about the Higher Power I know who I am sure can help you right now.

Tyler, I have enclosed some writings I did for situations just like this, when someone is questioning whether or not to believe in God. I want you to read these pages several times and ponder their meaning for you. I am not asking you to just start believing, but I do want you to think about all that has happened to you and how following your own set of rights and wrongs has caused you and your family a great deal of pain. The reason God has tried to reveal to us the right way to live is to prevent that very pain. You are a unique creation of God, designed in His image and given some very special talents He wants you to use for the good of mankind. By striving to do just that, you feel good and valuable and loved because you know you are doing the RIGHT thing. Going against this Devine process is guaranteed to cause failure and pain. You are experiencing that pain right now. Do you like it? I bet now.

God's love is unconditional. That means, there is nothing, and I mean nothing, that you can possibly do that will make God not love you. Oh we can disappointment Him, and we all do that on a regular basis. But, He is always there, waiting and wanting to help us. We just have to ask. You see, God does not intervene in our lives unless invited. It is quite simple, like talking to your earthly father. You just need to speak to him, in your own way, and ask Him to help. Trust me, He will.

God tells us that live will not be easy, and He is not going to miraculously make your problems go away, but He does promise good from any bad. That means Tyler it is not too late to turn your life around and make good of the time your have left. You do have a future, but the type of future is in your hands. You can continue to try and go it alone, or with the help of your dead dog, or you can seek the help of the real living God and start down the road of recovery knowing you have the most loving and all powerful father on your side.

I will continue to pray for you Tyler. I hope in some way this letter helps you come to understand an easier way to live your life. May God give you peace now and forever.

Doc Joe

APRIL 25, 2005 (11TH GRADE)

At the expulsion hearing, Ron and I were told that if we seek inpatient treatment for Tyler, he would not be expelled for his senior year. He is expelled from April 26 to June 8, 2005. He can take summer classes to make up his credits for this year. Praise God!

I don't know if it made a difference or not, but I took in some artwork to the expulsion hearing. I wanted the strangers sitting around a table making decisions about my son's life to understand that he is a person, an artist; someone with talent and not just some crazy kid who used drugs in English class . . . I wanted to personalize the situation . . .

END OF APRIL (11ᵀᴴ GRADE)

Dear Tyler,

I am so glad that you are in the hospital where you are safe and cared for. I hope that perhaps, they can find a medication that can help you with your depression and anxiety. If that's the case, perhaps you won't want to use anymore. I pray that is the case. We need help here. We may need a miracle. I'm not sure what we need, but I hope we obtain it with this current plan in place. I will never give up on you, Tyler, no matter how old you live to be or what your life entails . . . I know how you were raised, how much you are loved, and what kind of person you are at the core. I love you so much, Tyler.

Love,
Moo

MAY 3, 2005
(11TH GRADE)

Dear Tyler,

I am so glad that you are finally in a reputable rehabilitation facility that has the potential of helping you with your drug addiction issues. Bassett House seems like such a nice place and everyone seems knowledgeable and helpful. I hope that you get the most out of it that you possibly can. I hope that it will help you turn your life around. I hope that you will gain insight regarding yourself and that you won't want to do drugs anymore. I hope that you will see, by living with and listening to your peers, that you have a very good life and that you will want to honor yourself and your family by abiding by the law and living a legal life. I love coming and visiting you. That one time, when we brought Vinnie with us, so that the two of you could see each other, you were both so happy! I didn't realize that many addicts use with their pets, as some of the leaders explained to us. I loved how the lunch ladies told me that you are one of their favorite kids because you talk to them, and are so kind and polite. THAT is who you are! I want everyone in the world to know that part of you, as that's what I believe is the true essence of who you really are. It is weird around the house without you. I miss you. But I'm so glad that you're safe and cared for and getting the help that you need. This is an expensive program, but we can make monthly payments until we pay it off. It will take several years to do that, but I am not worried about the money; I just want you to be healthy and happy. That is all I have ever wanted for you and Seth-to be healthy and happy.

Love,
Moo

5/12/05   8:30am

My tenth day has just begun. ▓▓
is leaving today at 10:00. I feel awful. I
want to come home, but at the same
time I want the help. I miss home so much
I just want to scream. It seems like everyone
here is leaving soon except for me. I hate
it. And then also I don't know why I
want to be out so bad when that
would put me closer to my court date.
I'm just so afraid of going back to jail
or DYS it makes me cry just at the
thought. I'm feeling something that I've
been trying to put into words - but I
don't know what it is. I just feel different.
I think I'm upset about something, but
it's nothing I've written about above.

Letter from Bassett House

time: Sometime after
date: 5/13/45

Dear Moo Moo and Sasha,

were in the holding room right
now. I'm one of two white kids out
of eleven. Doesn't really make a difference
though because he's just as ghetto
as the rest of them. One kid is in
here for murder. I heard one raped
his sister. The kid I kind of made friends
with (_____) was part of an armed
robbery. Most of the others are here
for TV. I get made fun of a lot,
one kid even called I was gay. I'm allowed
to check out books and read, so I
plan to do that and also be on my
best behavior to get to "level II"
where I am allowed a five minute
phone call a week. All we do is watch
boring movies; I try to sleep. all the
chairs are metal, some kids play cards.
I am not a minority here, I am an
alien. I never thought it possible
to miss home so much. Tell seth and
Vinnie I say hi.
Enough about this place. What are
things like at home? I wish I was there.
I'm crying right now but I'm doing
my best not to let anyone see. I
now know the value of having to learn
a lesson the hard way, that's for
sure. Although I still am prepared for
inpatient, I feel confident in telling

you that I will never be involved
with anything illegal again. This
is single handedly the worst
experience I have ever had, and
it's only just begun. Plus those
kids are bad people I never want to
end up anything close to being like
them. I'll never mess up again. I don't
ever want to come back to this place,
ever it's awful. I hate everyone in here,
they're assholes. one kid after I got
here beat another kid into submission
and he was beat up so bad he was
sent home for two weeks just to recover.
I'm trying to stay on the beater's good
side, the best way to do that is not
talk, at all. so far (second day) I have
only talked to _____ (armed robbery kid)
once and the kid who called me gay once.
other than that I speak to no kids.
one kid was trying to take my trial
papers from me to see what I was in
here for. if I didn't love you guys so
much I would want to i.e. I actually
filled out a questionaire and now I
think I am on suicide watch Don't worry
though, I'm not going to harm myself.
Tell Seth I watched Malibu's Most Wanted,
he might think that's funny; all
the kids here loved it. We sleep on
plastic boxes with a "mattress" on top.
which is really a thin blanket. 2.

we wake up at 5:30 AM and go
to bed at about 9:00. I'm in what's
called "overflow" right now which just
means all the regular rooms are taken
up. The regular sections called pods
do activities like gym, art and they even
go to school. Since they are always doing
something taking up all the space, overflow
sits in the holding room all day. Literally
all day. It's a nightmare. The food is
so gross I can't choke it down, I just
don't eat. I drink my milk and I ate
the pineapples I got as a side to what
looked like a pizza but I'm not sure...
I do 250 crunches a day and 50 push
ups. When I come out I might actually
have a halfway decent body. I really
don't know what else I have to say...
I have set up meetings with the counselor
here once a day just so I can get
away from these ~~people delinquents~~ animals.
She's very nice, her name is ▓▓▓▓▓.
I can't wait to see you guys at visitation
tonight. I think it's some time around
3:45. There's no clock. I'm in prison.
It's a scary thing to think about. I'm
in prison. And it's so scary to think that
~~to~~ the day I'm released I could go straight
to Department of youth services for up
to like two years. If that happens I
literally think I might die. I think about
dying a lot in here, until I realize how

self sh it would be. I think about
what it would be like if I was dead
and what it would do to the family
and I began to cry. I've been crying
the whole time I've been writing this
letter pretty much. I don't miss my
friends as much as I thought I would
which kind of scares me. I don't have
many real friends. The only people I
miss are ████ ████ ████ and
really that's about it. ugh... Sometimes
I think about running away. It would
never work. (I have to go pee be back
in 5 mins).

They all are calling me bookworm
now... I don't mind being the only
decent poison in here though... It's
really weird. One kid even asked me
to help him read a letter he got one
kid asked what "deceitful" meant.
Hardly any of these kids go to school.
I suppose this is all I have to say
for now. I'll give you this at visitation
tonight so I can mail my one letter
I get to write a week tomorrow. This
is the only way to pass the time.
If you haven't already (I'm assuming you
didn't) don't tell any of my friends that
ask where I am. OK I'm out of room!
I love you all.

Love,
Tyler

"WHO AM I?"

Your self-concept is made up of all the images you have of YOURSELF.

Understanding your self-concept is a first step toward appreciating how unique you are.

This helps to build your self-esteem!

On each line below, answer the question, "WHO AM I?" in a different way.

Your answers can include descriptions of any aspect of yourself, including family and social roles; beliefs and values; what you like and dislike; talents and skills; or physical, mental emotional and social traits.

EACH RESPONSE IS A PART OF YOUR SELF-CONCEPT.

1. I am a son
2. I am a libertarian
3. I am an atheist
4. I am an artist
5. I am creative
6. I am open-minded
7. I am a go-getter
8. I am social
9. I am sensitive
10. I am a person who loves to learn
11. I am a good friend
12. I am a role model
13. I am sentimental
14. I am myself

The Baggage Cart

What baggage are you carrying?
  STRESS, guilt, shame, sadness, loneliness

How long have you been carrying it?
  Since about age thirteen

Who packed theses bags?
  I did

Do these bags still serve a purpose?
  Not Really

What bags do you want to carry with you?
  tools + skills and a few select beliefs + feelings

What feelings would you prefer to be carrying with you?
  more Positive ones.

What bags are you willing to let go of?
  almost all of them

What tools/skills do you have to help you in your recovery?
  strong will, Resilience, Courage

Do you need to acquire some new tools that you never
acquired before?
  Probably

Why I Deserve Role Model

I have been hoping to change my
life for a long time now. Now that I'm
getting all of this help, maybe I actually
will. When I get out of here I plan to
join lots of extracurricular activities,
run, and fill other aspects of my life
with something positive. It will be a pretty
easy thing for me to drop using friends
because I don't have any really, maybe
one or two. But the point is, I am
ready and willing to do whatever I can to
become sober. I realize the life I have
been living will lead me to a cell or
a premature death, that's not what I
want for myself, and I am ready to
change.

I think I deserve role model because
starting from day one, I have busted
my butt in treatment. I've participated
in group and caused minimal disrup-
tions. I've learned a lot here and I
think anyone in here would tell you
the same thing. Unlike a few people
here, I have taken all groups
seriously, not slacked off, and
I have absorbed all of the new
information. I think my behavior
shows that I am ready to become
a role model. I have gotten three
"1's", of which was contraband
found in the room whose fault is not
mine. Another for a towel out of
place, And a minor i for subgrouping.

So overall, in the 17 days I have
been here, I think I have proven I can
do what it takes to be on role model
level.

- **What is life to you?**

  life is the period of time from birth to death in which we have the choice to do with it what we plan

- **What is struggle?**

  an obstacle of any sort. The struggle is the process of overcoming it.

- **Name three things you can not let go of.**

  knowing I let my family down
  thinking I have failed

- **What holds an addict back from change?**

  fear of giving up control

- **Name one thing that you often deny.**

  that I am an angry person

- **List some things you have lost because of drugs**

  hope, junior year, friends, trust
  money, respect, freedom

- **Name one thing you wish you could change about your family.**

  nothing.

- **How can we get control back over our lives?**

  by first giving it up

- **Is denying really easier? Or does it only come back to you?**

  denying is ignoring, ignoring means eventually, it will grow out of control if it isn't already

- **Why is not having a sexual relationship important while trying to get sober?**

  because we could substitute the drug with the relationship

- **What is freedom?**

  the privilege of doing what you feel is appropriate.

June 6, 2005 (Summer before 12th Grade)

Dear Tyler,

I am so glad that you are finished at Bassett House and are coming home today. You seem so much more at peace. You've gained weight and you seem more content and relaxed than I have seen you in a long time. I am so glad that you got a lot out of the program and that you have vowed to never use drugs again. It is good to hear you say that you realize what a wonderful family that you have, and that you want to be a better son and person. Now, we just have to get these classes finished. I have paid for all of the classes, books, and so on, so you have to do the work. Some of it will be online and some of it will be at Rockbridge. I hope that you take the work seriously and do your best so that your GPA won't suffer too much, as you prepare to go to college. I am hopeful for your mental, physical, and emotional health, Tyler. We have done a lot to help you and now you must help yourself. Please do it.

Your Moo

REINSTATEMENT/PROCESSING FEE

PAYMENT INSTRUCTIONS

IMPORTANT! TO ENSURE PROPER CREDIT TO YOUR ACCOUNT YOU MUST:

- ◆ Make your check or money order payable to:
  OHIO TREASURER KEVIN L. BOYCE

- ◆ **DO NOT SEND CASH**

- ◆ Write your check or money order number in the box provided on the front of the fee payment receipt

- ◆ Write your BMV account number on your check or money order

- ◆ Do not staple your check or money order to the payment coupon

- ◆ Do not include additional correspondence

DETACH THIS PORTION AND MAIL WITH YOUR PAYMENT

REINSTATEMENT FEE PAYMENT RECEIPT   BMV 2005 07/07

BMV Account Number:	018616211
BMV Case Number:	XXXXXXXXX
Reinstatement Fees:	$125.00

20090722

Check Number: ☐☐☐☐

Money Order Number: ☐☐☐☐☐☐☐☐☐☐

XXX

Amount Enclosed: $☐.☐☐☐.☐☐

☐ Check **only** if address is incorrect
Print correct address below

2 OHIO BUREAU OF MOTOR VEHICLES
0 ATTN: RE FEES
0 P O BOX 16520
5 COLUMBUS OH 43216-6520

Name _____

Street _____

City _____ State ____ Zip ____

AUGUST 19, 2005
(FIRST DAY OF
12TH GRADE)

Dear Tyler,

Well, you are officially a senior in high school. You finished all of your summer school classes (this was no easy feat . . . I got stared down by an administrator one day while I was at your school getting some necessary papers, I had to beg/coax/threaten you to do your schoolwork, I was constantly bugging you about your academic timelines), and while your GPA doesn't really reflect how smart you are, you should still be able to get into college with no problem.

Your court hearing today went well. The two minor misdemeanors of disorderly conduct that you were charged with is a minor offense considering what it could have been. We owe the attorney so much money, but I'm not concerned about that right now. I'm just so relieved that a good decision has been made. Now, you have to do your thirty hours of community service, and return to court in about 180 days. Please just get this community service completed and do not get into any more trouble, Tyler. Please, please, please! I cannot take any more of this and I'm pretty sure your dad and Seth can't either. I know that we cannot afford any other unnecessary court/attorney expenses, and we need to move on and get into a "better place" within our family. Tyler, please make this last year a good one.

Relieved and yet anxious,
Moo

October 2005 (12th Grade)

Dear Tyler,

Are you serious? We found pot, a straw, urine, and cocaine in your wallet and in your bedroom. I thought that we were done with this crap. What do we do now? Yes, you always say that it was a one-time thing and that you're done with drugs, but the evidence proves otherwise. We have strapped ourselves financially to help you, and are at our wit's end with all of your shenanigans. Just do what you're supposed to do at school and at home and leave the damn drugs alone! Come on, Tyler! Work with us here. This is getting ridiculous and we are very frustrated with you! You keep lying over and over to us. You are not trustworthy. We did not raise you to lie. This is your family—the one who has done everything to help you. Be honest! What will you do in life? Will you ever get it and keep it together?

In anger and frustration,
Moo

November 2005
(12th Grade)

Dear Tyler,

Why are you having so many migraines? We are at the doctor constantly. You need to take the medicine that Dr. Merryman gives you. Are you faking these headaches or are they real? What is wrong with you Tyler? You have so many problems and it is really wearing me down. I want to be strong for you, Tyler but I am tired. I am tired, frustrated, stressed, worried, and drained. This is hard, Tyler. I am always worrying about if and what and how many drugs you're taking. I worry about the possibility of an overdose, and what damage these drugs are doing to your internal organs. I worry about whether or not you will land in prison, and most of all, I worry about whether or not these drugs have changed your thinking to the point that you're not the same person in your heart/soul/core that you once were. Are you still a good person, Tyler? A good person who is making bad decisions? Is this a temporary situation or a permanent one? Are you an abuser of drugs or a true addict? I know about addiction. I know what it is and how it works, and the fact that once you're an addict, you'll always be an addict. Will you be able to move past all of this? Are your migraines a separate condition or are they a result of your drug use? I don't know what's what anymore.

So confused,
Moo

November 2005 (12th Grade)

Dear Tyler,

I am so sad. I cannot believe my mom died so suddenly. Here, everyone thought that she had pneumonia and she died five days later from cancer. The doctors said she had it in multiple internal organs, including her lungs. How could we have not known? Why didn't she have the usual symptoms?

Thanks for flying to Florida for her service and then driving me back with her things. Since Dad had to go into a facility, as he cannot care for himself, we had to go through all of her things in the house. It was so hard, but I'm so glad that you were there with me. I have been so close to her my entire life and I just can't believe she's gone. She died so fast. I'm glad that I was there with her, along with my two siblings, when she died.

This has been a terrible year. I feel Empty. Depleted. Lost. Done.

So empty,
Moo

November 27, 2005

To Members of the Selection Committee:

I am writing on behalf of Tyler Harrison, who I have worked with since September of 2004. I feel that Tyler's academic record does not adequately reflect his true academic capabilities. Last year, Tyler made some poor decisions that resulted in him being expelled in April for the remainder of the school year. As a result he received a "WF" in each of his courses which counts as an "F" towards his cumulative grade point average. Our district has a replacement credit policy, in which we allow students to retake a course and replace the grade as long as they have improved the grade. The lower course grade does not count into their cumulative grade point average. As a result, Tyler worked very hard this summer and completed three courses through three different independent study options to utilize the replacement credit policy. He also is currently re-taking Chemistry, Painting and Pre-Calculus to improve his grades and to complete the course curriculum. Plus, he has a full course schedule to keep himself challenged this academic year.

Tyler has sought out new opportunities as he wanted to do something to help others. One of his after school activities is that he is serving as a mentor for an elementary boy to help discover his artistic skills. He enjoys troubleshooting computer problems for his friends and family. Due to his computer abilities he was asked by a teacher to develop a website for a newly-formed organization. Tyler is very passionate about his art and greatly enjoys the ability to express his creativity abilities. I feel that Tyler has made some positive changes this year and is striving everyday to continue in that direction.

Most importantly, Tyler is a genuinely a nice person with a lot of potential. He possesses many attributes which will make him successful in whatever he undertakes. Lastly, I feel very strongly that when he begins in a new environment he will flourish.

Sincerely,

School Counselor

Dec. 15, 2005

To whom it may concern,

It is a great pleasure to recommend Tyler Harrison. Tyler is a unique young man who displays a lot of promise in the arts. I definitely feel he would be a positive addition to your institution.

Mature ideas, ability and a great work ethic are a few traits that help Tyler to be successful in the arts. When ever Tyler begins a project, he puts a great deal of thought into the process. Tyler wants his works to truly represent the assignment yet incorporate his thoughts and feelings. Tyler's art really does parallel his personality. His work is extremely tight and precise, yet sometimes possesses a mysterious side. Tyler has always shown great ability in my class. From the very beginning Tyler's work seemed advanced and extremely detailed. Because of this, Tyler worked at a slower pace than most of the class. However, Tyler always put in extra time at home or during free periods to stay up with the rest of the class. This extra effort has taught Tyler a work ethic that will definitely pay dividends in the future. Lastly, and most important, Tyler has always treated me and everyone in my class with respect and friendliness. Tyler listens to advice, gives constructive suggestions and sets a great example for other students with his work ethic. Tyler's attitude has always been a positive addition to who he is as a person.

I am very excited about Tyler's future. With his combination of creativity, talent and hard work, Tyler will find a way to be successful. It is for these reasons I recommend Tyler Harrison for your school.

Sincerely,

Art Educator, Dublin Scioto High School

February 6, 2006
(12ᵗʰ Grade)

Dear Tyler,

Finally! Your last court hearing! Your records are expunged and to anyone who looks at them, you have no record whatsoever. We will be paying for years and years for your inpatient treatment, and we had to get credit card advancements to pay for the attorney fees, but it's all so worth it if you don't get into any more trouble or harm yourself any more by doing illegal drugs. I hope, because of everything that you and all four of us has been through, that you are motivated to do what's right. I don't think I can do all of this again, Tyler, so I sure hope it helps! I love you so much and I want the world to know that you are a good, talented, person. I want them to know how smart and skilled that you are!

Love,
Moo

7929 Stanburn Rd
Dublin, Ohio 43016

Amber L. Prekler
KSU Admissions Counselor
Admissions Office
PO Box 5190
Kent, Ohio 44242-0001

Dear Amber,

On 10-23-05, I applied to KSU by sending you a hard copy of my application. A few weeks ago, I received a letter from you stating that you had not received my admission fee. I had thought that I had submitted my payment online. However, since there is no record of my payment, please accept the enclosed $30 application fee. Please place this payment with my application.

I am very interested in attending KSU next fall '06. I am mailing a copy of my H.S. transcript as well as my letters of recommendation.

Although my cumulative grade point average is below your required standard, I am hopeful that you still consider me as a fulltime art student for next year. Most art colleges recognize that high school is not a good "fit" for many art students and I believe that I am one of those students. Last year I experienced several traumatic events and as a result, I failed my junior year. I am back "on the right track", however, and re-took three courses from last year during the summer. Only two of those classes, English and History, have been substituted for my failing grades from last year. My final math grade is forthcoming; I'm expecting to earn a B in the course. Additionally, I am retaking 2 classes from last year during this school year, one of which will be finished after the semester. I have a solid A in the semester class and the other is a yearlong class in which I am earning a B. When my math, art, and chemistry grades substitute for the F's that I earned last year, my GPA will be increased. The other classes I'm taking this year will also improve my GPA, as I'm currently earning a 3.0 or higher.

I am now focusing on improving my Art Portfolio for submission into your school. I have a pencil drawing, two charcoal drawings, an oil pastel drawing, an oil painting, and a sculpture in it at the present time. I'm adding additional pieces as I continue to take three art classes, one of which is an Art Portfolio course. Some of my artwork will be placed in the upcoming Scholastic Art Awards Show. Additionally, at least one of my pieces will be displayed in an art gallery in Columbus' Short North district in 5-06.

I look forward to hearing from you regarding my application to KSU. Thanks in advance for your time and consideration.

Sincerely,

Tyler J. Harrison

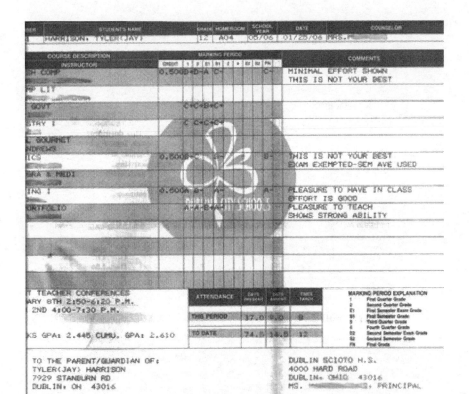

	STUDENT'S NAME	GRADE	HOMEROOM	SCHOOL YEAR	DATE	COUNSELOR
	HARRISON, TYLER (JAY)	12	A04	05/06	01/25/06	MRS. P

COURSE DESCRIPTION / INSTRUCTOR	CREDIT	1	2	E1	S1	3	4	E2	S2	FN	COMMENTS
SH COMP	0.500	B+	D-A	C-						C-	MINIMAL EFFORT SHOWN / THIS IS NOT YOUR BEST
AP LIT											
GOVT		C+	C+	B+	C+						
STRY I		C	C+	C+	C+						
L GOURMET NDREWS											
ICS	0.500	B-		A-	B-						THIS IS NOT YOUR BEST / EXAM EXEMPTED-SEM AVE USED
RA & MEDI											
ING I	0.500	B+	A-	A-	A-					A-	PLEASURE TO HAVE IN CLASS / EFFORT IS GOOD
ORTFOLIO		A-	A-	B+	A-						PLEASURE TO TEACH / SHOWS STRONG ABILITY

Y TEACHER CONFERENCES
ARY 8TH 2:50-6:20 P.M.
2ND 4:00-7:30 P.M.

KS GPA: 2.445 CUMU. GPA: 2.610

ATTENDANCE	DAYS PRESENT	DAYS ABSENT	TIMES TARDY
THIS PERIOD	37.0	9.0	8
TO DATE	74.5	14.5	12

MARKING PERIOD EXPLANATION
1	First Quarter Grade
2	Second Quarter Grade
E1	First Semester Exam Grade
S1	First Semester Grade
3	Third Quarter Grade
4	Fourth Quarter Grade
E2	Second Semester Exam Grade
S2	Second Semester Grade
FN	Final Grade

TO THE PARENT/GUARDIAN OF:
TYLER(JAY) HARRISON
7929 STANBURN RD
DUBLIN, OH 43016

DUBLIN SCIOTO H.S.
4000 HARD ROAD
DUBLIN, OHIO 43016
MS. _____, PRINCIPAL

*GRADING INFORMATION ON REVERSE SIDE

KENT STATE
U N I V E R S I T Y

February 15, 2006

TYLER J HARRISON
7929 STANBURN RD
DUBLIN OH 43016

Dear Tyler:

Congratulations! I have the great pleasure of informing you of your admission
to Kent State University. You have selected a university of challenging
academics, varied campus life, and rich diversity. We eagerly anticipate the
beginning of your college career at Kent State.

Details of your current status are listed below. Please review these items to
make certain they are correct. (Many of these are explained in more detail on
the back.) If you find any errors, please contact us in the Admissions Office.

Admission Type: New KSU Student
Term of Admission: Fall   2006
Major: Fine Arts

College/School: College of Fine and Professional Arts
Sex: Male
Permanent Phone: 614-766-8034
Residence Status: Ohio Resident
Social Security Number: 273-88-9164

Information about residence hall living will be sent to you by the Department
of Residence Services. If you have any questions about university housing,
please contact Residence Services in Korb Hall, (330) 672-7000. Details about
advising and scheduling opportunities will also be mailed to you.

Welcome to Kent State University. Please let us know if we can help with your
transition to college.

Sincerely,

Nancy J. DellaVecchia
Nancy J. DellaVecchia
Director of Admissions

FEBRUARY 2006
(12ᵀᴴ GRADE)

Dear Tyler,

You did it! You got into the college that you most want to attend, Kent State University! Oh Tyler, I am so happy. I believe that going away to school to study art, something that you are so talented at and have such a passion for, will be the new start that you need in life. You will meet new people, others who are similar to you and who are interested in a lot of the same things that you're interested in. You can share your past with others if you want, but you don't have to. You can be whoever you want to be at KSU. Although I will miss you, it will be great for you to live on your own, away from us, but not too far! It will give us all a break. I am just thrilled!

Love,
Moo

March, 2006

To Whom It May Concern:

I have had the pleasure of working with Tyler Harrison in the Art Portfolio class of Dublin Scioto High School for the past year.

In that time I have seen Tyler Mature and develop into a student who is able to channel his many creative ideas into his work. I have seen great growth in his ability to further define and give depth to his personal style of art. He is always ready to try new techniques and materials in his projects and is very focused when working. He has an eye for detail and patience to execute fine craftsmanship.

He is a soft spoken, hard working and dedicated young man. He is always open to direction and is very teachable. And better than that he is funny. His dry sense of humor is a pleasure in the classroom. I will miss his wit next year, but hopefully you will enjoy it!

Tyler has been the recipient of two art awards this year. He had a piece selected for the prestigious Governor's Art Show. And he received the teachers selection for the Ohio Capital Art Conference. I would highly recommend him to your program.

Sincerely,

A.P. Art Teacher

YEAR	STUDENT'S NAME	GRADE	HOMEROOM	SCHOOL YEAR	DATE	COUNSELOR
I	HARRISON, TYLER (JAY)	12	A04	05/06	04/05/06	MRS.

COURSE DESCRIPTION INSTRUCTOR	CREDIT	1	2	E1	S1	3	4	E2	S2	FN	COMMENTS
SH COMP	0.500	D+	D+	A	C+					C+	
HP LIT					C+						STUDENT IS PLEASANT AND FRIENDLY NEEDS TO PARTICIPATE MORE
GOVT		C+	C+	B+	C+	B+					
STRY I		C	C+	C+	C+	B+					
GOURMET					A						STUDENT IS PLEASANT AND FRIENDLY EFFORT IS GOOD
ICS	0.500	B+	C		B+					B+	
RA & MEDI					A						INTEREST SHOWN EFFORT IS GOOD
NG I	0.500	A	B+	A+	A					A+	
ORTFOLIO				A+	A+	A+					

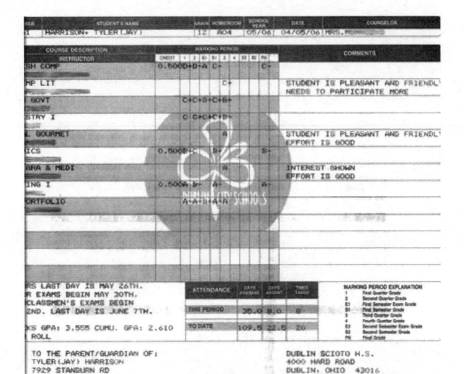

RS LAST DAY IS MAY 26TH.
R EXAMS BEGIN MAY 30TH.
CLASSMEN'S EXAMS BEGIN
2ND. LAST DAY IS JUNE 7TH.

KS GPA: 3.555 CUMU. GPA: 2.610
ROLL

ATTENDANCE	DAYS PRESENT	DAYS ABSENT	TIMES TARDY
THIS PERIOD	35.0	8.0	8
TO DATE	109.5	22.5	26

MARKING PERIOD EXPLANATION
1 First Quarter Grade
2 Second Quarter Grade
E1 First Semester Exam Grade
S1 First Semester Grade
3 Third Quarter Grade
4 Fourth Quarter Grade
E2 Second Semester Exam Grade
S2 Second Semester Grade
FN Final Grade

TO THE PARENT/GUARDIAN OF:
TYLER (JAY) HARRISON
7929 STANBURN RD
DUBLIN, OH 43016

DUBLIN SCIOTO H.S.
4000 HARD ROAD
DUBLIN, OHIO 43016
MS. MARINA DAVIS, PRINCIPAL

*GRADING INFORMATION ON REVERSE SIDE

May 2006
(12ᵀᴴ Grade)

Dear Tyler,

My heart is bursting with pride. You actually were formally invited and recognized at Senior Honor Night because of your artwork. You got to hold your head high, walk up on that stage of your high school and be recognized for who you truly are—an artist. NOT for the mistakes you've made—taking drugs. I couldn't be happier and more proud. It felt so good to have you and your work be honored. You so deserved it. You worked for hard that and have been trying to turn things around and you did it. You truly did it!

Love,
Moo

MAY 2006
(12ᵗʰ GRADE)

Dear Tyler,

Wow! You got to display your artwork in a REAL studio in the art district of Columbus! It was so cool and I'm so happy that some of my friends could come and see you, as well as your work. What a neat night! You looked so "in place" and "at home" in that art gallery amidst your beautiful sculpture, drawing, and stamped artwork. I know that you have worked really hard this year. You've achieved so much, especially after the year you had last year! You've produced some good artwork, finished school, earned recognition for your work . . . I'm just thrilled. My heart is lifted and feels lighter than it has in a long time. I'm so happy for you and proud of you, Bud. I love you!

Love,
Moo

We ask that you, as the artist, do not submit any artwork copied from published, photographs, magazines or illustrations of others artworks (see the rear gallery regarding copyright/fair use).

This is my original artwork (please sign) _____ and I release photographic rights to the Ohio Governor's Youth Art Exhibition. This includes the right of the Exhibition to post my artwork on its website. I also understand that I must assume the full responsibility for insuring my artwork.

Student
print or type
Home Address

Grade (circle) 9 10 11 (12)   Home Phone   Region # ___1___

School Dublin Scioto High School   Teacher

Title of Work TWO GRAMS OF REGRET

STATE cut here ————————————————————————————— cut here STATE

Student
print or type
Home Address

Grade (circle) 9 10 11 (12)   Home Phone   Region # ___1___

School Dublin Scioto High School   School Phone

School Address 4000 Hard Rd   Dublin   43016

Teacher   Principal

Superintendent   School District Dublin City Schools

School District
Address

Title of Work TWO GRAMS OF REGRET

Medium Charcoal   Category Drawing   Size 31 1/4 x 22 3/4

Tyler Harrison
Dublin Scioto High School
"Two Grams of Regret"

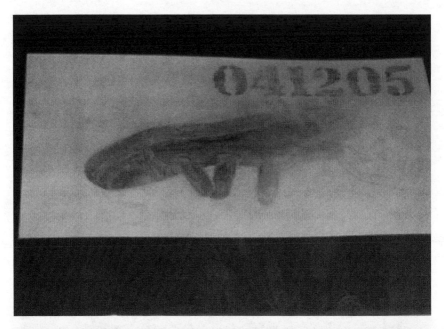

June 3, 2006
(H.S. Graduation Day)

Dear Tyler,

Congratulations! You did it! You graduated from DSHS with your class, even after having to make up most of your classes from last year. I am so proud of you, Tyler. To go back and face everyone who was talking about what you'd done (mostly rumors with some truth imbedded) was so very brave of you. Not only did you graduate today, but you went out with some honored art pieces. You worked hard and it paid off. To watch you walk across that stage with all the other kids in your class and take your diploma, just like all the other kids, meant the world to me! Now, you can move on from this chapter of your life to something new. You can create yourself in whatever way you choose at KSU. I know that you are very talented, Tyler, and if you apply yourself, you will go far. The world is your oyster, Tyler! You can do and be whatever you want. I am so excited for you, Bud. I love you.

Love,
Moo

AUGUST 2006

Dear Tyler,

I have mixed feelings after dropping you off at college. I wish that Dad could have come but since Seth was sick, we thought it best that I take you by myself. I am excited for you to start college and prove your talent and worth to others, as well as to yourself. I am excited for you to be around other people who have similar interests and talent as you. I want you to find your place in this world and to find a sense of accomplishment, happiness, and peace as well. I have high hopes for you, Tyler. I hope you get along with your roommate and make some good friends. Please enjoy school but take it seriously. Please do not start off college by getting into trouble or using cocaine or other deadly drugs, Tyler. Please start off on a positive note. You have so much talent, intellect, charm, personality, and are attractive. You will have fun but just pace yourself and don't go wild, Tyler. Please.

Love but nervous,
Moo

December 2006

Dear Tyler,

While your grades from fall term don't indicate a high academic standing (2 Cs, a B-, a S and a withdrawal), at least you passed all of your classes with a C or better and made it through the transition from high school to college. Given all of your issues, I think that you did pretty well. You only came home a couple of times. I know that you wish that you and Allyson were at the same college, but you can see her on breaks and on weekends sometimes. I hope that your relationship with her will propel you to work hard and finish strong, so that if the two of you are still together in a few years, you can build a life together as educated adults with degrees. You will have so many more options that way. Please finish strong this year, Tyler and give your classes your best next term. I am so glad that you are living away at school now. It has given me, your dad, and Seth a break from all of your issues that have plagued all of us for so long. It has been nice to focus on Seth this year, watch his freshman team win the football championship, and spend some peaceful time at home. I miss you when you're gone, but I don't worry quite as much about you when I don't see you every day and live with you.

Love,
Moo

JUNE 2007

Dear Tyler,

While I am not sure how you failed art history, I am glad that you finished this term with 2 Bs and 2 Cs. I am thrilled that you made it through your freshman year of college, and that you seemed to learn and enjoy the experience so much. You made a few good friends it seems (mainly girls—again, just as in high school), and are happy to still have Allyson as your girlfriend. Please make this a good summer for all of us by working fulltime and not getting into any trouble. I really need to have a good summer and I know that you want that as well. I am proud of you, Tyler, I truly am. You have overcome so many life obstacles already at nineteen. You have learned lessons that some adults never learn. I hope that you remember all that you have learned and merge it with your many talents to do something meaningful in your life. I know that you still have anxiety and migraines, and I'm sure that you dabble in drugs now and then, but you seem to be so much more level headed and optimistic about your future. Although I am still somewhat wary about you and your choices, I am a little more relaxed and confident about your future. That is a big relief, Tyler, it truly is. Keep up the good work!

Love and prideful,
Moo

DECEMBER 2007

Dear Tyler,

A third speeding ticket in a little over a year? Seriously? I am worried that you are going to lose your license, Tyler. Worse yet, I'm concerned that you are going to injure yourself or someone else behind that wheel. You need to slow down and obey the rules/laws. How is it that you only passed one class this term? What did you do all day if you stopped attending your classes? How many times did you speed down to OU to see Allyson? You are wasting our money and your time, Tyler, by signing up for classes and then failing to attend and finish them. What are you going to do with your life if you don't finish college, Tyler? I'm beyond aggravated, annoyed, and disappointed, Tyler. Get with it!

So disgusted,
Moo

KENT STATE.
UNIVERSITY

January 2, 2008

TYLER HARRISON
7929 STANBURN RD
DUBLIN, OH 43016

Major: ARTE
Student ID: 9164

Dear Tyler:

This letter is to inform you that you have been **continued** on academic probation at **level four** in accordance with the enclosed Academic Probation Policy guidelines. In order to avoid dismissal and to continue your studies at Kent State University, you must meet the following minimum grade point requirements:

1) Achieve a grade point average of 2.00 or above each term of enrollment until you are removed from academic probation.
2) In addition, within the next two terms of enrollment, remove yourself from probation or demonstrate academic progress by moving to a lower level of probation (see enclosed guidelines for probation levels).

All students on probation are expected to maintain regular contact with a faculty advisor and with the various student counseling and assistance services available in this office and at the university. As a condition of your probation, you must meet with your advisor each semester to plan your course work and to review your progress.

While you are on academic probation, you may not register for more than 15 credit hours, you may not register for courses under the pass/fail option, and you may not secure approval to take courses at another university as a transient student. If you are currently registered for more than 15 hours or are utilizing the pass/fail option, you must adjust your schedule immediately.

Finally, if you feel your probation is due to extraordinary circumstances and that personnel in this office should be aware of those circumstances, please call (330) 672-2780 to schedule an appointment.

Your faculty advisor and the staff of this office are available to assist you in a variety of ways. Please feel free to utilize these resources at any time.

Sincerely,

Nancy E. Mitchell, Ph.D.
Associate Dean

JANUARY 2008

Dear Tyler,

OMG! I cannot believe that you didn't go back to KSU. You are living in our home, working halftime at best, and causing us grief and havoc. I don't know where you are or what you're doing half of the time, and I can't believe that you quit KSU because you want to be near Allyson. She is still attending college fulltime, Tyler, and what do you hope to accomplish by staying at home? How are you going to fulfill your goals by sitting at home? You cannot just sit around our house, Tyler. You must work or go to school or both. I don't care if you take online classes or go to school somewhere in Columbus, I just want you to be productive with your life and more forward. Oh Tyler, I am so worried about you. I want you feel the worth that you have and prove yourself to you as well as the world. You have so much God-given talent that most people do not have. You need to use it. Please don't go backwards in terms of your recovery, Tyler. You aren't doing drugs again are you? Please say no . . . I am so distraught, Tyler . . .

So worried about you,
Moo

the confessions of a depressed boy.

WARNING:
nothing in this envelope is happy or uplifting
Read at your own Risk and with caution.

Wed, April 23, 2008. 3:06 - 3:53 am

dear mom,

last night i got a glass of milk with which to enjoy my
oreos. it was on my desk, untouched when vinnie jumped onto
the chair and his tail knocked it over all onto my laptop. i
acted quickly and did my best to drain the milk out of it
and took it apart to dry it off with a soft cloth i also used
compressed air to reach places i could not otherwise get to.
i unplugged it and removed the battery and disc reader.
it is currently upside down airing out. as of now (3:10am) it
still will not even turn on. hopefully by morning this will
change, but i won't get my hopes up. if it does turn on, there
will more than likely be additional damage (i imagine to the disc
reader lens and wiring, mostly) that will be relatively costly
to repair.

this is just the "green" cherry on top of my shit covered molding
chocolate brownie of a life. in case you haven't noticed, i'm not
exactly the happiest twenty year old on the block. i have more
things that make me want to cut off my own head than
you could possibly imagine. i'm severely depressed and much **MUCH**
more angry than you realize. out of all the problems i have,
the biggest one is the fact that i want to kill myself so bad,
but can't do it because i love my family and allyson too much
to actually do it. i think about it all the time. multiple times
a day. for example, i'm driving. i see a bridge with concrete
pillars holding it up. pretty much the only thing that keeps
me from gunning the engine and flying head on into it is the
mere fact that you and allyson exist. but i assure you, you
never have to worry about me doing such a thing so long as i
have your and allyson's love.

Why am i writing this? i'm not entirely sure. maybe
it's because you and i don't communicate as much as a
mother and son should. maybe it's the ink in this pen sloppily
creating the words on this page that help me vent which ultimately
directly aids in keeping me alive. who knows. the fact of
the matter is, i hate my life. I hate the way i look, i hate
the way i feel, i hate the fact that i constantly want to
be buried under the influence in an effort to never have to
feel. i resent happy people. how fucked up is that? i'm
so pathetic i actually hate people for being happy simply
because i can't be happy myself. I am not certain i've ████
felt happy ever and if i have, i don't remember it.

money doesn't buy happiness that phrase should end
with "just kidding." i don't want money, I don't want
or plan to be rich i simply despise the fact that how much
money you have directly relates to your social standing, your
level of influence and power, and your quality of life, which
directly translates to how happy you are. it's a broken
system in a broken world we live in an it makes me sick.
i bitch about ████████ getting everything she wants not
because i want what she has, but because she didn't do
anything to deserve it she was born, and has since
been given overstuffed handouts. i know i'm in a much
better situation than most people, but even that isn't
fair, which in turn makes me feel like even more
of an asshole. the most well-off people in the world
are born into a family with money, while the real heroes

like you and dad must struggle to live a mediocre life.

my unhappiness has led me into addictive behavior. i try to feel numb so i can avoid the pain i feel day to day. you know of two addictions i've had, well let me let you in on a little secret. i've been addicted to cocaine for a year in the past, i've been an alcoholic from senior year through freshmen year at kent, and i've also combatted a heroin and pill addiction (which was the **WORST** by the way) and none of them worked. currently i'm sober and honestly its not much better. this is the real world, and it sucks. its like a nightmare in which i'm on a terrifying rollercoaster lined with people armed with knives stabbing me as i go by. the rollercoaster leads directly into a brick wall and i can't wake up. pinch me, please. this really must be a dream.

Please don't cry. the last thing i want is for my pain to cause pain to those around me that i love. so please don't cry or feel sorry for me, none of this is your fault. in fact, it's all my fault. my views and unchangeable beliefs are what ultimately cause my pain. i do not like my life. i hate it. the best i can do is try my best to hate it as little as i can until the sweet release of death pulls me under.

                                Love,
                                (your failure)
                                tyler

i'm very sad today even more than usual, if you can believe
it. i was watching this show about the fifteen most violent random
acts in the US. the focus was all (mostly) about fucked up kids (male)
who just snapped and went on shooting rampages and killed tons
of strangers and then turned their firearms on themselves and i
realized as i was watching that i'm not sad that they happened
because of how violent and destructive the crimes were, but because
every expert would talk about warning signs the kids exhibited
and how someone should have seen it coming. i fit the bill. i have
just as many "warning signs" as these kids did, and what's worse, is
i think about things like that all the time. i think about going
on shooting rampages and then killing myself too. something about
how i have so much unexplained pain and sadness, and i feel like the
only way anyone could ever understand it is if i mercilessly murder
down total strangers and ruining lives to make more people have to
feel my pain would make me feel better. i think my targets would
be more planned, though, targets like ____ people that have caused a
considerable amount of my sadness. i want them to suffer. i guess
i'm just fucked up, but i have to go now. it's bedtime. hopefully i won't
wake up tomorrow and go on a shooting spree.

its the morning, and i am totally fucked. i'm so sick of having
more bills than most people have when they're 25. i'm only
20 years old. i shouldn't hate my life so much at all. i should be
having the most fun from now. i'm at the prime of my life and i can't
enjoy a single FUCKING thing about my life. i just want
to get hit by a car ~~_____~~

Wed May 14 2018 12:00

why can't i just be happy? i want more than anything to just be normal and happy. i'm no happier now than when i was addicted to drugs and before i met ____. shouldn't i be happy? i've got the best girlfriend in the world and i'm finally actually sober. why am i so sad? nothing will ever even me out. i feel like i'm so angry... so sad... all the time. i force smiles when i know normal people would smile, just so i can pretend i'm not as miserable as i am. i lie about how sad i am. i tell people that i'm feeling better and happier but really i'm not... i don't want people to feel sorry for me. i just want to be happy. most kids i know would wish for a new car of money or something like that if they had the chance. i'd just wish to be happy. i've forgotten what being happy feels like. hell, i forget what just feeling neutral feels like. i'm not even sure if i've ever felt genuinely happy, at any point in my life other than when i was just a small child.

JUNE 2008

Dear Tyler,

I am so glad that Allyson and you are going to be going to school in Columbus this fall and living together. You need to get back on the educational path, so that you can be a high school art teacher like you have always wanted to be. You have always been so great with children and you are so patient and encouraging. You will make a fabulous teacher! I know that you have missed living on your own and going to school. I know that you and Allyson missed each other very much when you were at two different colleges, five hours apart, so I am hoping that you will be happier and more focused when the two of you live together. Please stay on the right track, Tyler. I would rather see you go to CCAD but going to Otterbein is fine also. I just want you in school, working on your degree. Hopefully, most of your KSU credits will transfer, so that you're not in college forever.

I just want what's best for you in life, Tyler. You have so many endearing qualities and I really, really want you to be happy and healthy. I know that you have been depressed. I wish that I could wave a magic wand and make you happy. I don't know what else to do to help you. We've went to several doctors and counselors, you've tried a myriad of medications, we talk about your issues, and yet you don't seem much happier now than before we did all of that. I worry about you, Tyler. I am concerned that, with your being depressed, you will start using again. Please don't do that, Tyler. Things will get better. I promise. I love and believe in you.

Love,
Moo

DECEMBER 2008

Dear Tyler,

You need MORE money for school? Why can't you ever produce a receipt for these school supplies and books? When I give you this cash, I have no idea where the money is going. I need to see a schedule, an incomplete transcript, something that proves you are in school, Tyler. I need to be accountable to my family about where this money is going because we have lots of bills, Tyler, and other people need money in this family also. You always seem to put me in the middle, Tyler, and it's a stressful place to live. I'm always feeling as though I'm in the middle, trying to merge you—and sorta me—on one side with Seth and Ron on the other side. Please produce these receipts, Tyler. They are more than just pieces of paper. They are legitimate proof that you are going to school, that you are using money for educational purposes, and that it is being used for something positive. I cannot give you any more cash.

Always in the middle,
Moo

MARCH 2009

Dear Tyler,

What is going on with you? I help you get a job doing a mural for a teacher whom I work with and she is calling me all the time, saying that you aren't there when you're supposed to be. She says that it is taking you forever and that when you do show up, you don't work for very long. My reputation is at stake here, Tyler. I went out on a limb to get you some extra $$ for a job that you are more than able to do, and now you're being irresponsible. I don't know where you are; you don't live with me, so I don't know what you're doing. You seem to be going through a lot of money and now you're going to NYC with Allyson, so that she can interview for an internship. You're staying with your cousin and I really hope and pray there won't be any problems, Tyler. You kids are driving Allyson's car, and I pray that you won't speed or get into any accidents. You're behaving erratically, Tyler, and I am worried about you. You make all of these lists, but you don't ever seem to complete any of the tasks you've listed. Where is your transcript from Otterbein? Are you really in school? Oh Tyler, I hope you're not using again. I worry about you.

Scared/Nervous/Frustrated but still loving you,
Moo

APRIL 2009

Dear Tyler,

This has been a terrible month. First, you go to NYC and while you are gone, that teacher's husband calls me (the one whose mural you're painting in her sons' room) to tell me that you stole some of his pain pills. Apparently, he recently had surgery and has been at home recovering. I am not sure why he called me; probably because he can't get a hold of you. I am not sure how I am going to face this teacher again. Thank God, I don't work in her school anymore. I am so embarrassed and ashamed. Then, I find out that your cousin's roommate in NYC found heroin paraphernalia in their apartment. Are you using heroin? I'm sure that Allyson isn't. Heather says that she believes you when you say you're not using heroin, but also that you went from being sick when you first got to NYC, to being happy and well and in the meantime, syringes and other stuff was discovered. Now, there is a rift between your cousin and her friend. OMG! Tyler, if you are using heroin, this is very bad. It would explain a lot of things, though.

I cannot believe how much you cried when you came to see me in the hospital. You had gotten into that terrible fight with your dad and brother, and you said they told you that you are a drug addict, a thief, and a liar. Then you fell asleep beside me in my bed. The nurse let you stay way past visiting hours because you were so content and I was so happy that you were with me. Oh Tyler, are you using heroin? Are you using any illegal drugs? What is happening with you? I'm so scared for you, Tyler. I'm scared for your life, for your relationships, for your future. I'm scared for our entire family. I'm so scared that I feel numb, like I cannot move my left or right sides because if I do, something horrible may occur. I feel trapped and helpless and paralyzed with fear. Please be honest with me, Tyler. I cannot help you if you're not honest with me.

Love (but living in fear),
Moo

MAY 2009

Dear Tyler,

What is going on, Tyler? You ask us to attend an art show in which some of your work will be featured at Otterbein College and then when we are on our way to the show, you call and say that there was a fire and not to attend. Allyson told me that you told her that the art show had already taken place, and that we didn't bother to come. Why would you tell her that? Was there an art show? Are you even in school? Why would you tell your girlfriend that we didn't want to come to your show?

Now, Allyson is preparing to go to NYC for her internship and her camera is missing. Her mother is calling me, telling me that Allyson must take that expensive camera with her on her trip and I have no idea where it is. I have never seen that camera and know nothing about it. Where is it, Tyler? Are you stealing money from your girlfriend because you're using? Did you get rid of the camera, thinking that if she doesn't have it she won't go to NYC? Where will you live when she leaves? What will you do with that rabbit that belongs to the two of you? Oh, Tyler, where are you going in life? What are you doing with your life? I am so worried about you, Tyler.

I just want some facts even if it's information I don't want to hear,
Moo

END OF MAY 2009

Dear Tyler,

O MG! OMG! OMG! You're using heroin, Tyler. This is bad. This is really bad. We came to your apartment to move you home after Allyson left, and you convinced your dad that you needed $20 to pay someone back. You left the apartment that we were cleaning and when you came back, Dad walked in on you in the bathroom as you were shooting something into your veins. Is this where all the money has been going? Into your veins? OMG, Tyler, you are very, very sick.

I am thankful that you produced Allyson's camera, just in time for her to leave for NYC. I understand that she broke up with you, and that you used her credit card without her consent. She says that she owes several thousand dollars on her charge card and that most of those charges came from you without her knowledge. Is this true, Tyler? It's so frustrating for me, because I am trying to get to the bottom of a situation without sitting down to have a discussion with both of you at the same time. Allyson is in NYC, you are moving back into our home, you are depressed, your dad and I are already fighting about how to handle you, and here it is summertime, which I've looked forward to all year, and I can see it's going to be another bad one. I don't know that I can take another bad summer, Tyler. I am recuperating from that surgery and all kinds of stress, and I really just need a break. I feel as though I could lose it, Tyler.

If you are using heroin, I don't know what we'll do. That's the worse there is. Heroin? Really? If you're a heroin addict, I don't know what we'll do. Oh God, this is terrible . . .

Scared to death,
Moo

6.14.09   1:44 AM   Tyler Jay Harrison

I am a 21 year old male born and raised in
an upper middle class suburb of Columbus Ohio.
I grew up in a very nice house that my parents
worked so hard to make and keep that way. I
got decent grades all the way up until junior year
of high school. I'll skip all the things that we all
know all too well concerning drugs, and skip
straight to the point. I have wonderful parents
who have loved me and supported me my entire
life. I grew up in dublin. I'm not physically
deformed or mentally challenged, but for
some reason, I am **incredibly** depressed,
angry, suicidal, and

ABSTRACT DRIVER RECORDS

License/ID No. SS718797   [Login/Logout] [Services Menu] [Contact Us]

This is not an official BMV abstract. Click here for instructions on how to obtain an official BMV abstract.

Your Ohio driver abstract spans the previous three-year period.

License Status as of 07/22/2009: SUSPENDED   [View your reinstatement requirements]

ENDORSEMENTS: NONE

RESTRICTIONS: NONE

**************WITHDRAWALS**************

FRA REQUIRED UNTIL 07/10/2012

NC NON COMPLIANCE SUSPENSION   STATUS: SUSPENDED
    START: 07/10/2009 END: 10/08/2009   BMV CASE: NC09070281
    FRA START: 07/10/2009 FRA END: 07/10/2012

**************CONVICTIONS**************

C1 IN-STATE CONVICTION
    COURT: FRANKLIN CO MUNI COURT   COURT CASE: 9144563
    OFF. DATE: 05/05/2009 CONV. DATE: 05/27/2009 POINTS: 02
    OFFENSE: SPEED
    057 MPH IN A 40 MPH ZONE

C1 IN-STATE CONVICTION
    COURT: MORROW COUNTY COURT   COURT CASE: 59112007TRD7361
    OFF. DATE: 11/15/2007 CONV. DATE: 12/14/2007 POINTS: 02
    OFFENSE: SPEED
    079 MPH IN A 65 MPH ZONE

C1 IN-STATE CONVICTION
    COURT: FAIRFIELD CO MUNI COURT   COURT CASE: 7D00336
    OFF. DATE: 01/08/2007 CONV. DATE: 01/23/2007 POINTS: 02
    OFFENSE: SPEED
    074 MPH IN A 60 MPH ZONE

C1 IN-STATE CONVICTION
    COURT: FAIRFIELD CO MUNI COURT   COURT CASE: 6D10162
    OFF. DATE: 10/13/2006 CONV. DATE: 10/23/2006 POINTS: 02
    OFFENSE: SPEED
    097 MPH IN A 65 MPH ZONE

**************ACCIDENTS**************

A1 ACCIDENT DATE: 06/04/2009 COUNTY: FRANKLIN   BMV CASE: 98091171

END OF DRIVER RECORDS

OHIO DEPARTMENT
OF PUBLIC SAFETY

OHIO BUREAU OF MOTOR VEHICLES

HENRY GUZMAN, DIRECTOR   TED STRICKLAND, GOVERNOR

REINSTATEMENT REQUIREMENTS

License/ID No. SS718797   [Login/Logout] [Services Menu] [Contact Us]

*** NOT AN OFFICIAL BMV DOCUMENT ***

License Status as of 07/22/2009: SUSPENDED   [View payment instructions / coupon]

Your driver license expiration date is: OCT 15 2012

You have no driving privileges.

You are required to pay a total of $125.00 reinstatement/processing fee.
Please submit your check or money order, made payable to Ohio Treasurer,
Kevin L. Boyce, with the enclosed Reinstatement Fee Payment Receipt,
BMV-2005 or BMV-2007. Please DO NOT SEND CASH.

BMV CASE NUMBER:RC09070251 - NON-COMPLIANCE SUSPENSION
OFFENSE DATE: MAY 01 2009
SUSPENDED JUL 10 2009 TO OCT 08 2009
$125.00 REINSTATEMENT FEE REQUIRED
MUST FILE SR22 OR BOND UNTIL JUL 10 2012

For additional information, please call the Ohio BMV at 614-752-7500.

June 2009

Dear Tyler,

I'm very sorry that you lost your license as a result of that car accident, but I'm just glad that you and the other guy in the truck were not hurt. I know that this is bad timing, as you are already "down and out," but I will drive you where you need to go, and hopefully, you can get it back soon. I so want you to be healthy and happy, Tyler, and it's obvious that you are neither. I know that you want to hear back from Allyson, but there's a good chance that you won't. I don't know what all happened, Tyler, but it sounds like you owe her money and that you were using a lot of drugs when you lived together. Please get your transcript from Otterbein, as I really want to see what classes you took and what grades you earned. Please try to get a job. Let's all try to get along in the house this summer, Tyler. This is the last summer before Seth's senior year and I just want us to all enjoy each other.

Love,
Moo

AUGUST 2009

Dear Tyler,

A heroin addict? Is this what you are, Tyler? OMG! I am not believing this. I don't know that I can take it anymore. I'm just so tired and drained from all of this drug use, up and down, over and over, Tyler. Please, please, get the help that you need from Neil Kennedy. I know that you were mad when they transported you to the hospital from our house when you overdosed (again . . .) because I told them that I feared you were suicidal. I know that you didn't want to spend a couple of nights in the hospital, but I think it's for your own good. At least now, you've been accepted into a drug rehab center right here in Dublin. I didn't even know that it existed. I have talked to so many people and taken you to all these doctors, but no one ever mentioned this facility. I hope and pray that you get the help that you need. I hope the other three of us get the help that we need too, Tyler. This is so hard. We didn't raise you to be a drug addict, lie, steal, and betray the people you love and who love you. Please be the good person that I know that you at your core, Tyler. I still love you very much, but I am so very worried about you.

Love,
Moo

NEIL KENNEDY RECOVERY CLINIC	CLIENT NAME: Tyler Harrison
CLIENT PROBLEM AND TREATMENT PLAN	CLIENT NUMBER: ▓▓▓

Treatment Level Program: Partial Hospitalization	Plan #: 1

Problem (s) Description: 1. Opioid dependence; cocaine dependence; sedative abuse. 2. Depression DO NOS, anxiety DO NOS- per client report;; impulsiveness; emotional instability (aggravated by addiction). 3. Relationship issues. 4. Lack of sober supports.

How Was Problem Identified: initial assessment

Date of identification: 08/17/09

Client Strengths *Problem Solving Assets*	Client Weaknesses *Barriers to Problem Resolution*
Willingness; both externally and internally motivated.	"Fear of sobriety"; denial; anger.

Desired Behavior Change(Goal): 1. Establish abstinence. 2. Identify and address triggers, cravings, urges, and high risk situations. 3. Identify and address primary support group issues. 4. Address negative self image, impulsivity, and emotional instability. 5. Develop sober support system.

Anticipated Date When Behavioral Change Will Occur: 09/04/09

Objectives Client Will Complete to Obtain Desired Behavioral Change *(Those objectives necessary for discharge eligibility must be marked with an *)*

	Date Identified	Date Completed
1. * Start a recovery journal. The journal is maintained on a daily basis, and is checked weekly. Bring it to group each session. Contents include: all written treatment plan assignments; discussions about experiences with triggers, urges, and cravings; "lessons" from twelve step meetings; session notes; etc. Due: 09/04/09	08/24/09	___
2. * Establish a clean recovery environment by removing all drugs, alcohol, paraphernalia, etc. from home/living space. Compose a statement about when and how this was accomplished, and include a personal pledge to maintain it that way. Signs and date that statement. Due: 08/26/09	08/24/09	___
3. * Compose a written goodbye letter to your drug/drugs of choice. Due: 08/27/09	08/24/09	___
4. * List in writing three personal emotional "obstacles" to recovery and propose how to address each without using. Example: Anger- "I used to use when I got angry. Now I use a breathing exercise to help stabilize myself." Due: 08/31/09	08/24/09	___
5. *Describe a plan in writing for telling people- particularly those closet to you- about your recovery. Include an explanation for why you won't tell some people. Due: 09/01/09	08/24/09	___

1

NEIL KENNEDY RECOVERY CLINIC
CLIENT PROBLEM AND TREATMENT PLAN

CLIENT NAME: Tyler Harrison

CLIENT NUMBER: 94702

Additional Objectives (Continued from front page)

6. *Obtain a minimum of ten phone numbers from people who can serve as sober supports. Due: 08/04/09	08/24/09	———
7. * List in writing three personal triggers and three personal high risk situations. For each item listed, describe in writing a recovery strategy and/or method for addressing it. Due: 09/02/09	08/24/09	———
8. * Complete a chemical use history in writing as a timeline from birth to the present. Due: 09/03/09	08/24/09	———

Interventions Provided By Staff to Influence Behavioral Change:

Interventions	Frequency/Duration	Staff
1. Provide 1st Step Education x	2-3x weekly x	DDR
2. Provide Relapse Education x	3x weekly x	DDR
3. Provide Group Therapy x	Each day of treatment x	DDR
4. Provide Individual Sessions x	PRN x	DDR
5. Provide Case Mgmt. x	PRN x	DDR
6. Provide Crisis Intervention x	PRN x	DDR
7.		
8.		

Date the problem was resolved:

If problem was not resolved, describe the resulting plan of action:

I acknowledge that I have reviewed this treatment plan, have had an opportunity to discuss it with my counselor, and agree to follow this plan.

Anticipated Date When Behavioral Change Will Occur: 09/04/09

Client Signature _____ Date: _____

Counselor Signature/Credentials _____ Date: _____

Supervisor Signature (when necessary) _____ Date _____

2

9/2/09 homework: write down your three biggest fears

2. My family not letting me be welcome in their home anymore.

1. Never getting to be with ▰▰▰ again. (including being friends or even being just on decent terms.)

3. Returning to my disease state. (active using state.)

Discuss your current living environment.

> Describe your current living environment.
>> o What individuals are in your environment?
>> o Are these individuals healthy for your recovery?
>>> ▪ Explain why or why not.
> What are some dangers to my sobriety in my current environment?
>> o Describe how these are dangers for you.
>> o What can you do about these dangers?
>> o How can you cope with these dangers?
> How can I make my environment healthier for me?
> Describe some of your feelings concerning your environment.
> Describe sources of support that are outside of your environment.

My current living environment is my parents house. I live with my mother, my father, and my brother. They all can be healthy but in someways some of them really understand why, and they can all be supportive and understanding, but also they can be very not understanding and can actually be a setback in my recovery. Some dangers for my sobriety in this environment are triggers. When my family is not listening to me + I feel out of control that is a trigger. It's also been the setting for a lot of previous drug use. I can find healthy ways to deal with those things (music, skateboarding etc.) I feel that the people in my environment, while they can be supportive, can sometimes have a fucked up way thinking what the best way to help me is. I think they could all benefit from some type of education on how drug addiction works + what it is. other sources of support include my best friend ____ Thats about it.

OCTOBER 2009

Dear Tyler,

I know that you didn't really want to go, but I'm so thankful that you did agree to go to inpatient rehab at Neil Kennedy in Youngstown. I know that you don't want to spend your birthday there or really be in rehab at all, but we all agree that is the best place for you. You need help, Tyler. You need more help than what outpatient or Doc Joe can provide. It was so kind of Doc Joe to get licensed to dispense Suboxone to help you with your heroin addiction, Tyler, and maybe his help will be sufficient in the future, but right now, you need more intervention than going to his office once a month. Your counselor at NK advised me to start "letting go" of you, Tyler, because he says that eventually, you will either die or be in prison. I refuse to do that, and I think it's terrible that a counselor would advise that. Even if it is the truth, I do believe that I will see you on the other side of your addiction. I hope and pray that's the case anyway. I believe in you, Tyler. I want to help you. I will never give up on you. You are my son, you are a good person down deep, and you don't want to be this way. You don't have to be this way. I love you, Tyler. Please help yourself. We will come to Youngstown to participate in family group sessions, Tyler. Please give this intervention 100% of your energy, emotion, and time. Please focus on your recovery and nothing else. This may be your last chance to do an inpatient program Tyler. Please give it your best shot.

Love,
Moo

A COMMON MISCONCEPTION ABOUT LOVE IS THE IDEA THAT DEPENDENCY IS LOVE. ITS EFFECT IS SEEN MOST DRAMATICALLY IN AN INDIVIDUAL WHO MAKES AN ATTEMPT, GESTURE, OR THREAT TO COMMIT SUICIDE OR WHO BECOMES INCAPACITATINGLY DEPRESSED IN RESPONSE TO A REJECTION OR SEPARATION FROM A SPOUSE OR LOVER. SUCH A PERSON SAYS, "I DO NOT WANT TO LIVE, I CANNOT LIVE WITH OUT MY BOYFRIEND/GIRLFRIEND, I LOVE HIM [OR HER] SO MUCH." AND WHEN WE RESPOND "YOU ARE MISTAKEN; YOU DO NOT LOVE YOUR BOYFRIEND/GIRLFRIEND."

"WHAT DO YOU MEAN?" IS THE ANGRY QUESTION. WE TRY TO EXPLAIN" WHAT YOU DESCRIBE IS PARASITISM, NOT LOVE. WHEN YOU REQUIRE ANOTHER INDIVIDUAL FOR YOUR SURVIVAL; YOU ARE A PARASITE ON THAT INDIVIDUAL. THERE IS NO CHOICE, NO FREEDOM INVOLVED IN YOUR RELATIONSHIP. IT IS A MATTER OF NECESSITY RATHER THAN LOVE. LOVE IS THE FREE EXERCISE OF CHOICE. TWO PEOPLE LOVE EACH OTHER ONLY WHEN THEY ARE QUITE CAPABLE OF LIVING WITHOUT EACH OTHER BUT CHOOSE TO LIVE WITH EACH OTHER."

Mom & Dad

The desire to love is not itself love. Love is as love does. Love is an act of will- namly both an intention and an action. Will also implies choice. We do not have to love. We choose to love. No matter how much we may think we are loving, if we are in fact not loving, it is because we have chose not to love and therefore do not love despite our good intentions. On the other hand, whenever we do actually exert ourselves in the cause of spiritual growth, it is because we have chosen to do so. The choice to love has been made.

END OF OCTOBER 2009

Dear Tyler,

Where are you? Why did you leave Neil Kennedy? Why aren't you answering your phone? Oh, Tyler, I so wish you would have stayed in rehab. Surely being there for twelve days is not enough. We worked so hard to get you in there and now you've walked out, and you said that it was helping you. Why Tyler? Why? Please answer your phone! I am sick with worry, Tyler. The people at the treatment center said that they were surprised that you walked out because you seemed to be immersed in the program, were participatory, and involved. They said you formed healthy relationships with others and then surprisingly just left. Oh God, Tyler, what now?

Sick with worry (again/still . . .),
Moo

NOVEMBER 2009

Dear Tyler,

Please learn a lesson about how precious life is from the tragedy that just occurred. Seth's friend and girlfriend died in that automobile accident. It happened in an instant. They weren't drinking or doing drugs or anything. But they also weren't wearing their seatbelts. Two good people—a kid that Seth has played sports with and known since kindergarten, a kid with such a nice family, a kid we have watched play sports for years. Our hearts are broken as a community. Please learn from this, Tyler. I never want to bury either of my sons. It would kill me.

Please don't die, Tyler. Please get well. Please, please, please . . .

Love,
Moo

DECEMBER 2009

Dear Tyler,

The unbelievable has happened. My great-niece, April, is deceased. Her six month old fetus is gone. Her parents and sister are heartbroken. Another death in our family—a death of a seventeen year old girl who was beautiful, artistic, and smart. A death of an unborn baby boy whose name was Landon. I am in such a dark place. First, there was the death of a boy that we intervened with so much at school last year, who died this fall, then Seth's friend and girlfriend died in the car accident, and now April and her baby. I don't know how I spoke at her funeral, but I'm glad that I got through it. I don't know that it was such a great speech, but I did it. I'm glad I was able to do that one little thing. I will never forget being at the hospital when they removed her life support. This is so hard.

Tyler, please learn from this situation. Please see how hard it is for us to lose April in our family and imagine the pain and suffering you would cause if you died. Please live your life to the fullest and stay away from potentially deadly acts. Just take yourself out of all those bad situations. Stay on the right track. Make something of yourself and with your life. I love you, Tyler. I'm so glad that you're alive, but I have to wonder why April died of a brain aneurysm and you, who have put so many illegal and deadly substances into your body willingly, are still alive? There must be a purpose to your life. Please find it and let that purpose propel you forward into positive action. Please, Tyler, please. I need you to be healthy and whole. I need you to be productive. I need you to be a good person. I need you to be alive.

Love,
Moo

m + dad,

I've decided I'm going to get back on suboxone. only this time, it will be legitimately prescribed (by Doc joe) and will be monitored by a professional + accompanied with counseling (by someone in Doc joes office.) I never should have stopped taking it so soon in the first place. I just was not and still am not ready to do this without the aid of medication. I respect Donn's philosophy that total abstinence is the way to go, but I do not think that its the best course of action for everyone, including me. Since I've been off of suboxone and at Neil Kennedy, I've had more relapses and several problems than when I was taking suboxone illegitimately. I simply don't think its the best way for me to conquer this addiction.

Since suboxone helps tremendously with cravings, as well as having Naltrexone in it, I believe it is better suited to help me than the Naltrexone shot alone (which does not help cravings) I will be willing to pay for my visits to Doc joe + my prescription if you want. I just wanted to write this letter to let you know that I will not be returning to Neil Kennedy, as I have already made my appointment to see Doc joe. (its on tuesday after my appt with _____) I hope this decision sits well with you, and you will continue to let me live at home for the time being. I have my best interests at heart and like I said before, I honestly believe this is the best way to go in order for me to get healthy. I will be more than happy to submit to random drug screens (suboxone does not show up as an opiate) to make sure I am not using any other drugs. I will also be attending AA meetings regularly, probably 2-3 times a week minimum. I hope you will support me on this decision because I can tell you right now that Neil Kennedy is simply not going to work for me. outpatient rehab has not worked for almost everyone I know who has done it. but suboxone has worked for almost everyone I know who has done it. Thank you for all of the care, support, and love you have given me so far. I'm sure if we can keep that up and get the suboxone program going, we can be on our way to having our family back with a truly, honestly sober me.

love,
Tyler

DECEMBER 2009

Dear Tyler,

I am sorry that living with your friend in Kent didn't work out for you. I know that you miss all of your friends at KSU, and I'm sure that it's difficult to see that they've moved on, graduated from college, are starting to get to jobs in their fields, and that you are "stuck" within yourself—within your addiction. I am also sorry that you have "burned bridges" with some of your friends by borrowing money and not paying it back; living with them, but then not paying your share of the rent because you are lying about having a job and money. Tyler, where are you going in life? I was so hoping that you would spend long, quality time at the inpatient rehab facility and get the help that you need. I really doubt that being there for less than two weeks is going to give you the reboot that you need to turn your life around. You are so talented, smart, cute, etc., but you are in a huge negative loop. You seem to be going nowhere in life and it breaks my heart. You have all of the talent/intelligence/skills that it takes to be super successful in life, but you aren't able to take the steps necessary to get there because of your drug use or whatever other reasons there might be that I don't know about. I look at you and I see sadness, despair, distraught, and hopelessness. All things that I don't want to see in either of my sons . . . And the hard part is that, I want so much to fix it—to make it better for you, to help you. I have tried and tried, and I truly don't know what else to do.

I feel so alone myself. All of my friends' kids are moving on in life. They're getting married. They're working in great jobs, making lots of money. They are buying houses. And I'm happy for every one of them, I truly am. I have no one to talk to in great detail about our situation. How do I explain something to someone that I don't even understand myself? How do I relate details about a situation when I'm not sure I have the correct details? Or even all of the pieces? Your dad is mad at you, your brother is sorely disappointed in you and I'm trying to make it "right" in the family—to keep peace, to keep us united, to be a "real" family. It's hard, Tyler. You're making it nearly impossible. Please help yourself. Do something. I'm fearful, Tyler. I'm scared "to the bone" as my mom used to say . . .

Feeling sad and scared,
Moo

January 2010

Dear Tyler,

I am glad that you are working in the bakery at Giant Eagle, Tyler. It's not a dream job, but you seem to enjoy it (except for working with that one lady that you don't really like), and you are making good money. You don't have a license or a car but I don't mind transporting you. Tyler, are you still using drugs? Please talk to me. Open up to me, even if you have things to say that I don't want to hear. I'm so worried about you. You will be sitting on the deck, playing WOW on your computer or on Facebook or whatever, and then all of a sudden your head is down and I realize that you are asleep. Are you not sleeping at night? How can you fall asleep as you're typing? Does this mean you're on heroin? I read about the nodding off side effect. I hope not, Tyler. I am so concerned.

So concerned,
Moo

March 2010

Dear Tyler,

Ifeel as though I am watching you disintegrate. You only have one friend who comes over sometimes. You don't go anywhere because you don't have any money, and you have no license. You do have a new girlfriend now that you seem to really like. She seems like a nice, innocent, young girl and while I'm glad that you have found someone to do things with, it scares me to think about what she might be exposed to or try because of knowing you. That is terrible to contemplate, as I know that you would never intentionally harm anyone, let alone someone that you love, but it's possible that it could happen accidentally. You loved Allyson for several years and so deeply, and that did not turn out well. The two of you never speak and you feel as though you have no closure because she left and went to NYC and you haven't spoken to her since. My heart is breaking because I don't see you producing much artwork, and yet, you don't work that many hours. You talk about art jobs as though they are "dreams" and not anything truly attainable. You don't talk about any concrete steps you're taking to achieve your dreams. There seems to be nothing concrete in your life; it's all ethereal. My heart is breaking just watching you sit alone for so many hours every day. How can I help you? What is the truth? Are you using or are you not? What are you thinking? Why aren't you improving yourself? What can I do/should I do to help you?

So devastated,
Moo

(Not sure of the date. This is a drawing of our safe. We keep all of our bank account information in here and lock up our billfold and wallet daily.)

June 2010

Dear Tyler,

I'm so glad that you have your license back and that maybe you can find another job. I'm still not sure what happened at Giant Eagle. You said that you have a lead at Subway. I sure hope so. You and Amy seem happy and I'm thrilled that the two of you are going camping this summer. You seem like you have some things to look forward to and your energy seems better. Does this mean you're no longer using drugs? I know that you're on Suboxone and you've been on Xanax for a long time. Are these medications helping you? Are you ok?

Love,
Moo

January 2011

Dear Tyler,

Are you truly going to get a manager's position at Subway? Is this where you want to be? Is this what you believe that you deserve? Is this the path that you want to stay on for the future?

I know that you are depressed a lot of the time even though you have a girlfriend and a job. I believe that you would be really depressed if you didn't have a girlfriend. You have very little money, so you don't go anywhere or do anything fun. I feel as though you are wasting your youth, your time, some of the best years of your life. I know that you say that you are "behind" your friends, in terms of your place/position in life but yet I don't see you take many steps to move forward—to catch up, to go somewhere. I don't hear about your goals or see you take action to reach any of them. I know that you don't want to be living in our house, and we want you to be independent as well. I don't see you working enough to be able to do that. Seth is living on his own and he's four years younger than you. When will you be independent, Tyler? These years just seem to be dragging on and nothing is happening. Nothing moves you forward, Tyler. Please do something to help yourself and change your current situation, Tyler. Please. For you, for me, for our family.

There is nothing wrong with being a manager at Subway. I don't really care where you work. All I have ever wanted for both you and Seth to be happy and healthy. If this job makes you be that, go for it. I just don't want you to give up on your dreams and aspirations that you've had for so many years. I don't want you to ignore your God-given talent and all of the wonderful traits that you have that could you lead you into so many different career paths. I don't want you to have vocational regrets when you're thirty, forty or fifty years old. I will support you, Tyler, in whatever you decide that you want to do. I want whatever you want, if it will make you happy and healthy.

Love,
Moo

May 2011

Dear Tyler,

Are you really going back to KSU, Tyler? With Amy? You say that you're applying, and meeting with people and trying to get financial aid, but are you really? We cannot support you this time, Tyler. We are tapped out financially. I am drained emotionally, and am still reeling from the fact that you were never in college when you lived with Allyson. All of that money that we gave you went for drugs. You say that you are past that but are you really? You and Doc Joe seem to have a love/hate relationship. You're in his Suboxone program and then you get kicked out. Then you're back in again. Do you get kicked out because you have dirty toxication screens? Are you using? I didn't think that you could use heroin and be on Suboxone at the same time. I still find burned spoons around our house. You always say that they're old ones, but I'm not so sure. We have replaced spoons for our silverware set three times because they always disappear. I know that's one of the ways that you use heroin, Tyler. Are you using now? How can you take Amy and go to college if you're using? Are you really going back to college? What is the truth, Tyler? I really need to know. How will you get your Suboxone if you're up in Kent? I have so many questions and concerns . . .

So anxious,
Moo

Untitled

dear moo,

i'm very sorry to have to tell you this, but i need to get it off of my chest. i'm sorry i can't really do it in person
face-to-face, but apparently that's just the kind of person i am; a coward.

i wish i was dead.

seriously.

i spend hours upon hours each day wishing i had never been born. wouldn't that have made your life easier? seriously.
i know it would have. you wouldn't have such a fuck up for a son. don't try to sugar-coat things either. i'm a loser.
i quit jobs(i can hear you on the phone with god-knows-who saying the same things.)
i have no work ethic. i've screwed over
almost everyone i've ever met at some pont.

my meds aren't working. i need serious long-term anxiety meds like valium for the rest of my life (which no doctor will
prescribe, because of my history,) or else i'm over 99% confident i'll end up killing myself.

i'm a sociopath. i'm a liar. i'm a thief. i'm just an all-around horrible excuse of a human being that's simply taking up
oxygen that decent people could be inhaling. i hate myself because of the decisions i've made in the past, and no matter how
hard i try, i can't seem to make things right.no one believes anything i say, so what's the point of telling the truth? i'm
100% certain that at the very least, dad and seth think i'm still using.(i'm not, by the way, but what's the point in even
trying to defend myself when no one even comes close to believing anything i say.)

i wasn't joking when i said i have a real gun. not a BB gun either. I have an H&K USP p2000sk compact hidden in one of the walls
of this house. it's loaded, too. and i'm dead serious.

help doesn't work for me. meds don't work. therapy doesn't work. i'm a lost cause that no one has any kind of faith in; including
me (not to mention my own family. but i honestly don't blame you.) i have no faith in myself. mainly because i don't deserve to
have any faith in myself. i'm lonely, depressed,and constantly on edge.i go to sleep every night praying to a god i don't
even believe in that he'll grant me mercy and just let me die in my sleep. that's the definition of pathetic.

i'm not sure if you've noticed, but this really is how i feel. i have ZERO motivation. why? because i don't plan on living past
the age of 40 or so, (and no one seems to believe that i have it in me anyway.) probably even earlier.
i have nothing going for me. i'm worthless. i'm an awful excuse for a human being and
if people like me didn't just kill themselves, evolution would end up taking steps backwards.

people like me NEED to be weeded out. we NEED to die. i'm so afraid of failure that i don't even try.i don't give a shit. what's
really sad is i know that i'm smart. i know i have an above average intelligence level. but i don't deserve it. when i was born,
it was some kind of awful cosmic prank of chance. i ended up being a drug addict who lies and steals from people i love. what good
am i to anyone if i don't even believe in myself?

July 2011

Dear Tyler,

I cannot believe the letter that you just showed me on your computer. You actually got enough financial aid to go back to college! I'm so excited for you! And Amy is transferring to KSU. KSU is always a place that you loved and felt as though you belonged. It's a good place. A good fit for you. And yet I feel somewhat uneasy. How are you going to afford this apartment that you just found? Granted, it's nothing spectacular, but it's certainly not free! We have no extra money to pay these expenses, Tyler. There are just so many unknowns . . . I want to be totally happy and excited for you but, if I'm honest, I will tell you that I have some doubt. It's so hard not to. We've done this so many times . . . It seems like we've done it even more times than we probably really have . . . But, I'm going to try to be optimistic. At least you're not just sitting around nodding off anymore. Hopefully, this will be the first step that you're taking to move forward in a career later in life. I know that you want to be an art teacher and someday own your own art gallery. I know that you want to live in a big city and create art. You have so many great dreams, Tyler, and they are all reachable. So perhaps this is the exact step that you need to take to make all of your dreams a reality. I hope so, Tyler. I pray to God this is the case.

Love,
Moo

8/15/2011

Dear Mom,

First of all, HAPPY BIRTHDAY!!! I sincerely hope it is nothing short of a perfect birthday. I hope you know that I really do love and care about you more than I can even express with words, despite the recent arguments we've had and some of the things I've said. For my entire life, I know that you also have loved me unconditionally and I know you have always given 110% to be a fantastic and loving mom, even though there have been times where I have not been a good son, or even a good person, for that matter.

It seems like most (if not all) of the letters I have written to either you or dad recently have been more focused on me and my recovery as opposed to being about the person the letter is to. But today that will not be the case. I will spend some of my time on that stuff but I feel that the bulk of this letter should be about you, how much I care about and love you, and how fantastic you are as my mother and as a person.

These past couple years have seemed like decades. They've just endlessly dragged on and on with seemingly no end in sight. But I feel like now, things are truly starting to _____ _____ _____ I have _____ _____ so with (in my opinion) and I want it to be known that you are by far the biggest reason for that. You have stood up for me and defended me when I didn't deserve it, and you've provided me with more help and support than you're even aware of, partly due to the fact that I have failed to show/acknowledge it, and for that I apologize. You have been like the all-in-one force for me. I feel like I have beaten all of the odds against me. I believe that because of you in large part, I am clean, not in jail or prison, and most importantly, alive. That doesn't even include the fact that now I feel infinitely better than I did a few months ago. I feel like I have went from feeling completely 100% hopeless, depressed, stressed out, and sure to fail and end up with no real life or future, to feeling hopeful, happier, much less stressed and I now believe that I do indeed have a future, and not just any future, a bright one, one that will make me happy and you proud. And it's because of you, mom. I needed someone to believe in me... someone to talk me through my frustrations and my sadness and you did. So you can celebrate your birthday today knowing that you've basically saved my life, even when I didn't want to be saved and just wanted to roll over and _____ _____

December 2011

Dear Tyler,

Your apartment expenses are killing us. Neither of you have jobs in Kent, and we keep taking money out of our home equity line to pay for your rent and utilities. Are you even in school? You keep saying that there's something wrong because your grades aren't posted, so you cannot prove to me that you're in school, but why can't you show me your schedule online? Amy says that you are taking classes, but then Allyson thought the same thing when you lived with her. Why don't you have a job? What are you doing up there? I'm willing to make the financial sacrifice if you're really in school and are moving towards earning a degree. I am just not convinced that is really happening.

Moo

CHRISTMAS 2011

Dear Family,

I write this letter to each and every one of you in hopes that we can reach some sort of healthy equilibrium. Some of you I have a healthy relationship with, others are borderline, and others hardly exist at all. And no one is more aware than me why that is. It's my own doing, really. But I feel the best thing that came out of _____ half-assed sermon tonight is that this year, in this family, we don't have to be worrying about the several issues that plagued our home for the past couple of Christmas seasons. I am healthy. I am clean. I am sober. I have gotten my ability to care about people and most importantly about my family, without whom I would surely be dead. Each of you had a significant impact on me to get my shit together and here we sit, with the year 2011 winding down and I feel as if I've done it in a very big way.

Now I'm not saying there isn't work to be done because certainly there is, also I'm not saying I deserve the credit for turning things around. There were times when I wanted to use. But when I thought of the family, and specifically thought of some of the faces/fights/etc that I gone on in the past, it wasn't even a close call. You guys have been my safety net, whether you realize it or not. I just wanted to write in this letter not only should we all be grateful at how far I have come but how far our family has come as well. And it's because no matter what, one way or another, we stuck it out. We did what we could only think to do and we used our best judgment. And I for one can't even begin to put into words just how much each and every one of you mean to me this holiday season. But damnit if I won't try.

Mom,

I don't really even know where to begin. Because surely without you specifically, I would be dead. You had so many impossibly decisions to make and you had to make them so quickly. And I must say you did an absolute bang up job. Especially with me kicking and screaming and fighting back any way I could the entire time. I'm sure that was just a living hell. I like to think that you and I have a close relationship. And aside from the past couple days when I felt like I was on a witness stand being cross-examined by district attorney, I think if we're not all the way back to where we should be/were, we're damn well on our way. I am very conscious of the sacrifices and I'm very aware of what you had to give up and the hard

FEBRUARY 2012

Dear Tyler,

OMG! You wrecked your car? Amy says that you are extremely depressed. I'm scared to death. I'm scared that you're going to try to harm yourself. What is going on up there in Kent? Oh Tyler, I thought that this was going to be a great year. I'm so worried about you. Please, please, Tyler. You have so much to live for. Don't harm yourself, Tyler. Let me help you. Let Amy help you. Please help yourself.

Love,
Moo

MAY, 2012

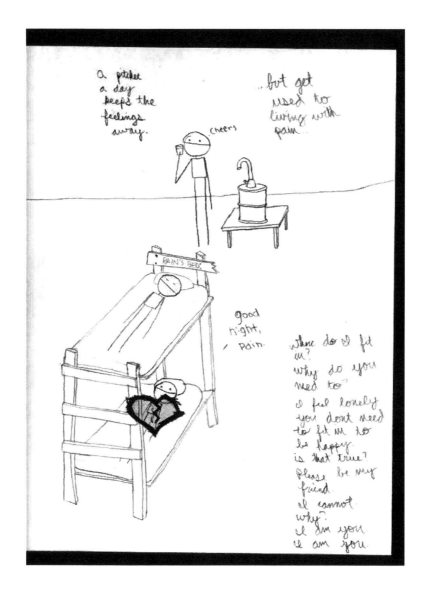

May 2012

Dear Tyler,

I cannot believe that you have lost your license again. They said there was some incident in Kent or Barberton. A theft charge? What did you steal, Tyler? My God, you know better than to steal. We went through thousands upon thousands of dollars to subsidize your living expenses up there, and you got financial aid to go to school, so why did you feel the need to steal? So because of traffic tickets, that accident that you were cited for, and now this mysterious charge for which I have no details, you have lost your license. Again. How are you going to work with no license? Are you going back to school in the fall? Where is your transcript? I still have no proof that you were even in school. Where is the TV that we bought you for Christmas? Did you pawn it like you have other things in the past? What is happening Tyler?

So now you are moving back home . . . OMG! I don't know that I will survive all of this. I really need to know what is going on, Tyler.

Moo

MAY 2012

untitled

i need to be on long-term anxiety meds. i'm developing severe agorophobia. i don't
even want to leave the house.i know what's out
there. what's out there is about 6 billion people that i have yet to screw over. and
i don't want to do it. but i also can't live
legitimately because when i try to, or even when i do, no one believes that i am.
including my own family.

i feel like i'm a child (and maybe i am..) that needs constant supervision and needs
to be reminded of the simplest things.
▬▬▬▬ ▬▬▬▬ had the right idea. he was one of the most intelligent people i've ever
had the pleasure to meet and converse with.
but he knew, just like i know, that once you're an addict on something as disgusting
as heroin, there is no coming back. no matter
how long you've been clean.

the best i can hope to achieve is a position at a job. not a career. a job. like a
cashier. and i won't do it. i won't live like
that. i'd rather be dead.

i should have never met ▬▬▬. she's the most beautiful person inside and out that
i've ever met. and she can DEFINITELY do better
than me. and she deserves better than me. she deserves someone that is an actual
decent human being. just like you, seth, and dad
deserve.

if i didn't have people in my life that actually cared about me, i'd be dead.
fortunately (maybe UNFORTUNATELY) i do have people
that care whether or not i live. but if the day comes where i truly believe no one
cares, or no one believes in me, i will be
gone.

and that is no joke. you can bet your bottom dollar. AND take it to the bank. that i
am 100% DEAD serious.

i hate myself. i hate the decisions i've made that i can't get past. and i hate
everything about the world around me.

based on all of this, can you honestly say that i'm a person deserving of the air i
breathe day in and day out?

i don't think so.

-tyler.

January 2013

Dear Tyler,

I am so sorry that Doc Joe died. I am so sorry for your extreme loss. Doc Joe was someone who always cared about, listened to, and tried to help you. He never gave up on you and he always tried to lead you to having a relationship with God. You and he had a love/hate relationship. You would be in his program and then you wouldn't be. You would argue with him and then the next time you'd see him, you'd come home and sing his praises. You loved to debate with him about philosophical issues. He loved you, Tyler, and you loved him. He became licensed to dispense Suboxone because of you. He has helped some of your friends and you have told everyone about him. He was a very important part of your life, especially these past four years since you've been a heroin addict. I'm so sorry he's gone. You were so worried about him and his cancer. You talked endlessly about him when he had stem cell replacement, and was in the hospital for so long. To beat all of that and then die of MRSA, well, that just doesn't even make any sense. It was such a shock to lose him after he was back to work fulltime and was cancer-free for the first time in several years. I'm so sorry, Tyler.

I wonder who will help you now? How will you get your medicine? Will you be able to stay clean so that you can continue to get your Suboxone? You have disagreed with and been through so many doctors, Tyler. I believe (although I really don't know for sure) that you've left doctors (or been kicked out?) because you didn't follow through or weren't there on time or perhaps tried to get extra medication. How will you keep a new doctor?

I worry about you, Tyler. You say that you can't go to the funeral home. I'm concerned that you will regret that, Tyler. I wish I was home this weekend to be with you, but this is our annual Hocking Hills weekend with all of our friends, and your dad and I both need this getaway. It's one of the few times we get away from the house together for more than a night.

Love,
Moo

MARCH 2013

Dear Tyler,

I am exhausted trying to help you. I truly am. I love you to death and would do anything in the world for you, but I am tired. You don't seem to be going forward in life. You are stuck. You've been stuck for a very long time. You aren't working consistently anywhere, you have no license, and every time we go to a courthouse up in Portage County or in Franklin County to get your license, they say that it's straightened out, but when we go to the BMV, there is always an issue. Some court appearance that you say you didn't know about, so you failed to appear. Some fine you didn't pay. Or the fine is paid but the court costs didn't get paid. So I make phone calls and all these notes and since they will never let us pay over the phone, we drive wherever and do this all over again. Again and again and again. You're depressed and I can certainly understand why. I think I'm depressed too. I feel as though we are mice on wheels. We just keep going around and around and around. We can't get off of the wheel and when we do, we end up back on it just to keep going around some more. It's terrible. I feel this huge weight on my shoulders and can't get out from under it. I want so much for you in life. You have so much innate talent and potential. You have more God-given talent than the vast majority of people. And yet the older you get, the less you art you produce. The less of anything you produce.

How can I help you, Tyler? How can I help myself? This new doctor, who they say is a temporary, doesn't want to prescribe your Xanax anymore. If you don't have that, you will be even worse off than you are now and I truly cannot imagine what that will look like. I called a colleague to get some names of psychiatrists to help you and you've been through two of them already. You always say there's some sort of problem and you can't go back. Are you even going to these appointments? What is really happening? I constantly bug you about giving me receipts and you have some of them for the doctor visits but not all of them. I have to give you cash but am not really sure how much the office visit costs and exactly where that cash is going. God knows I can't give you a check or credit card.

Sometimes, I feel as though I'm living in a nightmare and I can't get out. I feel trapped. I feel suffocated. And then one day, you'll be so happy and my heart feels hope and lifted, only to go back down again the following day. It takes a lot out of a person to go up and down like that emotionally, Tyler.

Please know, that no matter what you do or where you end up in the future, I will always love you. So much. So deeply. So profoundly, Tyler.

So tired,
Moo

July 3, 2013

Dear Tyler,

OMG, Tyler! You did it! You got your license back! I don't believe it! I'm so happy for you! And for all of us! Now, maybe you can get a job that you really like, get on the right path, perhaps go back to school. Oh, Tyler, I'm absolutely elated. I feel as though all things are possible. It took ONE AND A HALF YEARS to get this license back, Tyler. Don't lose it again. For God's sake, don't lose it again!

I can't believe that you and the BMV guy played that trick on me where you came into the building after you drove, looking all sad and then after what seemed like a lifetime but was probably only a few seconds, you both started smiling and laughing! I was so worried that you had done something wrong somehow and failed your driving test! Here you really passed, but you told him to go along with your joke!

So happy,
Moo

July 30, 2013

Dear Tyler,

How fun was today? I loved going to the Warped Tour Concert in Cincinnati with you today! The bands weren't that great but we had so much fun! We laughed and I drank (because you drove, now that you have your license again), and we laughed some more. I'm so glad that I had this experience with you, Tyler. Thanks for getting the tickets from your boss and taking me. I know that I wouldn't have gone had Amy not been working, but selfishly, I'm glad that it worked out like it did!

Love,
Moo

AUGUST 2013

Dear Tyler,

I'm so glad that you got that fabulous job in the Short North working for the lady who owns an art gallery! And to think that it's someone that my dear friend went to OSU and graduated with! Although when I told you that, I saw a momentary funny look on your face. I hope that doesn't mean that you don't actually have this job. You do work very strange hours and don't seem to have a set schedule. But I believe in you and am going to assume that you are being truthful. I'm glad that you are finally working in the art field. I really believe that this job can lead you places and could be an entry into the field that you were born to work in. I'm so proud of you for getting this job, Tyler. Now, I need to see some pay stubs! Prove yourself and your work experience, Tyler!

Love,
Moo

AUGUST 13, 2013

Dear Tyler,

I cannot believe that you totaled the Hyundai. That was a great car and I know that you feel horrible. I'm so glad and relieved that you didn't get hurt. I don't understand why someone would run you off the road and then just keep going without waiting to see if you got hurt, or even lived, for that matter. Was it intentional, do you think? I know that you are very shaken up. It's okay. I know that, since we didn't have collision insurance on the car because you boys have had tickets and accidents which makes our insurance rates sky high, you won't have a car anymore, but we will work something out, Tyler. Please stop talking about the "horror" of this accident. It's not horrific. It's an accident. Yes, financially, it will definitely hurt us, but I'm just glad you're not physically hurt. So, this business card of this truck driver you gave me, its legitimately someone who saw the accident, pulled over, and vowed to testify in your behalf or just reconfirm the details of the accident if your dad or I decide to call him? Oh Tyler, why do all of these things happen to you? You have had so many "horrific" experiences that were directly or indirectly caused by the choices that you made, but then you have other experiences that seem random and that you had no hand in . . . are they random? Are there people after you, Tyler? Have you screwed some people over recently? Ran some drugs and owe people some money, perhaps? I worry so much about you that it hurts, Tyler. It's hard for me to breathe sometimes, but I know it's not an asthma attack. It's like my throat is constricting on its own. My nerve endings feel like fireworks. I'm a wreck sometimes, Tyler—often, actually. Going to work and talking to "normal people" about "normal things" in their "normal lives" helps . . . it truly does. That's why I don't share many of these stories with my girlfriends either because I don't want to talk about this stuff all the time, as it makes me anxious, fearful, sad, and pessimistic. When I'm with my girlfriends, I just want to have fun and forget about the "dark world." The dark world of drugs, bad guys, guns, fake jobs, money of questionable origin, bit coin, silk road, prescriptions over the internet . . .

So worried,
Moo

148

AUGUST 2013

Dear Tyler,

When I stopped at the light at Stanburn and Hard Roads, and I saw a beat up, old car sitting across the street, my heart started pounding hard. I knew it was trouble. Sure enough, when I looked at our front porch, I saw a man banging on the door. I also saw a small statured person in the junker, probably a female. I knew right away that this man was your drug dealer. The drug dealer that you've talked about numerous times with me. You even say that he's a bad man, and I just knew in my heart who it was before I even pulled into the driveway. I rolled my window down as calmly as possible, trying not to convey the anxiety that I was desperately feeling, and asked, "May I help you?" to which he answered, "Are you Tyler's mom? I'm a friend of Tyler's and I've been trying to reach him all day. Do you know where he is?" Tyler, I know that you owe this guy money. I'm pissed, Tyler. You are putting all of us at risk with this drug shit and I'm getting really sick of it. We've lived like this for years and your dad and Seth and I don't do anything to deserve it. How much do you owe him? Why do you owe him? I hate that I even know how all this crap works. As soon as I saw that car, I knew he was at our house. I shouldn't have to live like this. I was on my way home from school, for God's sake, working with middle schoolers. I don't use drugs. I don't do illegal stuff (okay, yes, I speed in the car sometimes . . .). I don't want bad men with guns and vendettas, guys who are angry, knowing where I live and coming to my house. What is wrong with you, Tyler? I know that you love me and your family very, very much. Why would you do anything, even ONE THING, that would jeopardize our lives? Our safety? Our security? I'm uneasy living in my own freaking house in my own freaking neighborhood, Tyler and it's because of you. I'm angry, Tyler. I've been scared, worried, and a little mad before, but now I'm realizing how selfish your acts are. I know that you are an addict. I get that you hate your life and you don't want to be like this, as you've told me a hundred times, but don't drag your family down with you. It's bad enough that you shoot heroin into your veins but to risk the lives of your own mother? A person that I know that you love and care about very, very deeply? Come on, Tyler! Get with it! Stop this shit before we all get shot!

MOO

September 2013

Dear Tyler,

W hat does this letter mean that you got from the Doctor taking over Doc Joe's office? You are kicked out of the Suboxone program? For good? Who will be your doctor? How will you get your Suboxone? How will you get the Xanax that you've taken since 7th grade? Why did you get kicked out? Are you using again? Oh Tyler, I am so worried about you. I just don't know what is going on.

Why did you lose the job in the art gallery? You said it was because you didn't have a car and couldn't get there when they wanted. Well, now you have a vehicle again. Granted, it's not much, but it works! Do you think that you can get that job back? Why are you working in a pizza place? Why aren't you pursuing other art positions?

Where are you going with your life, Tyler?

Forever wondering,
Moo

OCTOBER 2013

Dear Tyler,

I'm sorry that your birthday was so lousy. I don't know why you and Amy broke up, but I can tell that you're very depressed and that you believe the break-up was your fault. I don't really want to know what happened, but I guess I want to be reassured that it wasn't something horrible that happened or that you did . . .

Who are these new girls that you are bringing to the house? You said that you met them in the hair place next to the pizza place? How? Why? I feel like every time you have a break-up you meet all of these new people in hope of starting over but it never ends well. Is Amy okay?

You said that you are working at Chipotle in Westerville and that the one girl is someone you work with. I get the feeling that you're not really working that job, Tyler. Are you?

Why don't you just tell me the truth? Haven't we been through enough crap over the last ten years that you can just admit when you don't have a job? How is it that you have enough money for cigarettes and gas if you're not working much or at all? Oh, Tyler, I so worry about you.

I see that you're getting your Xanax over the internet now. Are you getting other drugs over the internet also? What is Silk Road? I saw something pop up on my checking account that has to do with bit coin. Ron and I don't use bit coin. What is it? Are you accessing our checking account again?

When I try to talk to you about these issues, Tyler, you answer my questions with other questions. It's a strategy that you have used for years. We go round and round with no resolution to anything. It's very frustrating to me. And yet we can have the deepest, most profound conversations about other topics. Why can't we have an honest, deep conversation about what is happening in your life? I'm worried about you, Tyler.

Feeling like we're back on the roller coaster,
Moo

BEGINNING OF DECEMBER 2013

Dear Tyler,

Say what? You want me to go to church with you in Worthington to hear one of those new girls that are coming to the house sing? You've never asked me to go to church with you and you typically don't make friends who are churchgoers. I'm not complaining, I'm secretly thrilled, Tyler! But it is perplexing. You always keep me on my toes, don't you? You're always coming up with new ways to surprise me! About the time I feel as though I've seen and heard it all, you shock me with some new statement or request, such as going to a church we've never been to before to hear a girl that you just met sing a song. Do you like her? What about Amy? Amy's been coming to the house some also, but you say the two of you are just friends. How can you not be in love with her when the two of you have been together for several years? Are you sad? Are you happy? You seem pretty good. You look good and you seem as though you have good energy. Are you still working at the pizza place and at Chipotle? What are your future plans? What about the Suboxone? Do you need it? Are you trying to get it?

I feel so unsettled. I'm anxious. I try to be optimistic, but my history with you has taught me to be cautious. To be watchful and observant. To try to stay one step ahead of you, which I feel as though I can rarely do.

Seth is sick of living in our house because of the way that we have to lock everything down. It's hard pretending that we are a close family when there are so many hard feelings, especially on Dad's and Seth's parts. I don't blame them at all; I understand exactly how they feel. And yet, I won't give up on you, Tyler. I refuse to give up on you. I believe that you are a good person down deep. In your heart and in your soul. I believe that you can beat this addiction. That you can and will go places in life. You have so much to offer the world, Tyler. You care about the plight of others, even strangers. You are articulate, good looking, charming, intelligent, creative, and good with kids. You have so much to contribute to the universe, Tyler. You have so many people who love you. Please be on a good path, Tyler. Please. For me. For you. For the world . . .

Love,
Moo

January 2014

Dear Tyler,

I know that you are depressed and I'm sorry, Tyler. We had a good holiday and my friend who saw you on December 26 said that you looked better than you had in years. I agree with her, and yet now, you've taken a downward slump. I don't see the new girls or Amy coming around very much. I know that you've been talking a lot to your friend, and you say that you're going to work in the distillery that his family owns. You told me where it is, but I know that section of the city and I've never heard of or seen this distillery. You've never mentioned that his family has this distillery. I'm nervous, Tyler. Something isn't making sense. Why aren't you working in the pizza place? Why aren't you trying to get more art jobs? Why do I never see you producing art anymore? What is happening?

Love,
Moo

January 29, 2014

Dear Tyler,

You told me that you're sorry about what happened last night but I still don't understand it. You said that you met Nick for lunch today, as though you didn't overdose and almost die last night. Did you tell him what happened? Who are you being honest with? Anyone? You say it was an accident and that you didn't mean for it to happen, but why did it happen? Why are you using heroin again? Where are you getting it? How often are you doing it?

When we came upstairs to go to bed, your dad heard a funny noise in your bathroom. The shower was running and the bathroom door was locked. Even though we pounded and screamed, you didn't answer, and Ron said he continued to hear a gurgling sound. We broke the door down, to find that you had shot up and overdosed and were starting to turn blue. I called 9-1-1 while your dad did CPR on you . . . Something snapped in me this time, Tyler, and that's why I told you that we weren't going to the hospital with you and that you'd have to find your own way home. I told you that we're sick of it and that we're not going to do all of this anymore. Take you to the hospital, wait with you, bring you home, spend money on a bunch of doctors and medicine, only to have you shoot up and do it all over again. I am pissed. This is the first time I'm pissed about what you're doing, right at the time you're doing it. I've gotten mad before, but generally only after you are home from the hospital, and I know that you're okay. Now, I'm just mad that you're doing drugs at all. Period. Dad and I are nearing retirement, and we shouldn't have to live with this crap anymore. We have a broken bathroom door, you're using heroin, Seth moved out with a guy from work and his buddy, we have very little money in our savings, and it's just not where we want to be in life, Tyler. If this is how you want to live, you go ahead, but do it elsewhere. I'm serious, Tyler. I just can't and don't want to do it anymore. It's too much. It's gone on too long. I'm so tired. I'll never forget the policeman standing on my stairs, looking at me, and telling me that my son is going to die. They went into your bedroom and found all sorts of evidence that you've been using, Tyler. We used to search your room a lot and then finally stopped. What was the point? Every time we found what we thought was new evidence, you insisted that it was old and that you'd just "found it" in a bag you hadn't used in a while or whatever. How can we prove it's new or old? Why should we? I'm just sick of the same cycle, the same arguments, etc.

I'm serious when I tell you that I'm taking you to the homeless shelter to live if you're not living independently when Dad and I retire in the fall. You say that you and your buddy are going to get an apartment together but how can you do that if you're not working fulltime? You're twenty-six now, Tyler. You need to move on in life and live on your own.

I know that you hated seeing Apple Valley, which is where we are thinking of retiring. You said that the reality of all our lives changing in the next year when we retire is hitting you big time and that you realize things aren't going to be like they have. You're right. They are not. I am sorry that you didn't like Apple Valley, but dad and I are excited to retire and move and start a new life. I need you to get settled between now and October, Tyler. We are going to be selling this house and moving, and you are not coming with us. That's not much time, Tyler, for you to get working, save enough money to move out, and be settled. You better get a plan. You better act on that plan. Things are changing, Tyler, and you need to be independent. It is time.

Love,
Moo

January 30, 2014

Release . . .
RELEASE . . .
RELEASE . . .

Dear Tyler,

OMG! OMG! OMG! There is only one word in my head and I didn't put it there. RELEASE.

I wondered why you didn't answer my texts and phone calls today. My heart is broken. I came home from school and when I knocked on your door and you didn't answer, I went and got the key to your door and found you deceased in your room. I am numb. I am shocked. I am sad. I am so many things that I don't know what I am. You are gone. My beautiful, smart, savvy, creative, talented, caring son is gone. What am I going to do now?

RELEASE . . .
RELEASE . . .
RELEASE . . .

In devastation,
Moo

February 2, 2014

Dear Tyler,

Your memorial service is over. There were hundreds of people there. There were eight people who spoke so eloquently. A friend of ours played the guitar at the beginning and end. Pastor Lou led the service. We displayed all of your artwork that we could find and some friends helped us put together a video.

I'm so numb and tired and distraught that I can barely put one foot in front of the other. I forget to eat—that has never happened before. I cannot believe you're gone. I will write more to you later when I can sort out my emotions . . .

Love forever,
Moo

MARCH 1, 2014

Dear Tyler,

Oh, my dear son. I miss you so much. I miss seeing you. I miss talking to you. I miss hearing your voice. I even miss the messes you always left around the house. I miss your smile. I miss seeing your messy room (we cleaned it before company came from out of state for your service). Vinnie misses you. Dad and Seth are walking around sort of aimlessly. It's like we're all robots. I can't stand to sit at the table because your spot is always empty and just smacks me in the face like a huge semi. I miss hearing your music. I miss seeing you at your computer. I miss you smoking your pipe. I miss hearing you run up and down the stairs a hundred times a day. I wait for you to walk through that back door. I miss your text messages. I even miss your agony—you couldn't get your medication, you ran out of your medication, you are so behind your friends in life, you are sad, you are lonely, etc. I miss it all. No, I take that back. I don't miss the drug world. That dark, dark world that I never thought I'd see a glimpse of. I don't ever want to see any part of that again. That I don't miss.

Love forever,
Moo

July 30, 2014

Dear Tyler,

One year ago today we went to the outdoor concert in Cincinnati. We had a blast. Initially, in the car, I was talking to you about some of the many concerns I had about your behavior, if you were still using or not, if you were working real or fake jobs, but when you suggested that we table all of those conversations for another time and just have fun, I agreed and so we did! I laughed so hard, drank a few beers, and just enjoyed being with you somewhere fun, outside the house and away from everyone that we knew. We took pictures of each other and one of my all-time favorite pictures of you ever, as an adult, was one that I took at that concert. You took one of me laughing, after I'd drank a few beers, and assigned a specific ring tune to it (can't remember which one) and showed all your friends when I called you, the picture of me half lit. Remember how we hauled all of those chairs to the entrance from the car? Only to find out that there were seats inside, and you had to carry them all back to the car? OMG, I laughed so hard.

Tyler, I miss you so much but I can tell you that I don't miss all of the ups and downs that your drug-addicted lifestyle brought to our family. I will always miss you and I would never wish that you died, but when I am truly honest about how disruptive, bone-chillingly scary, and on edge I was for so long, I would tell you that it was not by choice to live that way.

One of the conversations that you and I had multiple times that stands out in my mind was when you told me that addicts hate being addicts. That you hated the way you were, and so wished that you could be the person that you were before you started using or any way that didn't represent or encompass an addictive personality. I was startled because you looked me in the eyes when you talked about this, and I knew that you were being 100% honest. You did not want to be an addict. You did not choose to be an addict. You tried not to be an addict. You were still an addict. The pull of the drug was so great for you that it made you lose everything and almost everyone (almost; one of your worst fears was losing your family but that never happened) that meant so much to you. You lost your pride, your self-respect, both of your girlfriends, countless jobs, endless amounts of money, your safety, etc.

The signs that you are alive and healthy keep me reassured and somewhat comforted. I'm still in agony every day over losing you though. You have appeared to multiple relatives and friends in dreams, telling them that you are happy, healed and healthy. You appeared to me twice in the same spot of the house in spirit form. I was so surprised the first time; I thought I imagined it, until you appeared again the very next day in the same spot. What is amazing is that, I read a book about spirits who visit us after they've departed this world and this expert said that, spirit forms almost always appear in our peripheral vision, generally over a shoulder and usually the right shoulder. That is exactly what happened both times when you appeared. I read the book after I'd seen you both times. It confirmed what I already knew. One of my girlfriends who knew and loved and cared about you very well/much saw your spirit on the front porch, sitting where you normally did with your laptop, the night of your service/wake when everyone came to the house. She saw you sitting there multiple times thereafter. Another dear friend who lives several states away went to a medium to connect with her mother who had died the month before you and after ten minutes into the session, the medium asked her if someone had just died tragically and she said yes. She saw you and described you as a "young man who was beautiful, intelligent, and very creative." You said that you were happy and healed and that you desperately wanted to get this message to us. You said that you were sending messages to us and that we should "look and listen." You also indicated that you were told "there would be no healing" for you in your physical life. You worked through the teacher at my school who had never used the Photoshop app before and had never met you. In order to design your CD memorial cover, you guided her and she told me that she knew she was being guided and that she felt as though she "knew you" by the time she was finished. I could go on and on about all of the signs, but the important thing to me is that you are still alive. I know in my heart that I will see you again and I know that you are no longer plagued with a disease that you hated. I miss you profusely, and I still get very sad at times and can cry at the drop of a hat, but I'm also comforted by knowing that you still exist. I cannot thank you enough for sending all of those signs, Tyler. And it's so like you to send them in a multitude of ways, through a variety of people, some whom never even met you!

Love,
Moo

December 30, 2015

Dear Tyler,

It's been almost two years since you died—in one month exactly. In some ways, it seems as though it was just a couple of months ago, but in other ways it seems like ten years ago. We've had so many signs in the past twenty-three months that you are still alive. Thank you, thank you for all of these. Going to a wedding in July when I was back in Ohio allowed me to meet a mystic. Someone who has helped thousands of people all over the world by conveying messages from loved ones. She told me that you did not mean to die, are trying to communicate with your dad and brother, she saw your girlfriend standing off to the side, separated from us, to whom you are also sending messages to, and she told me countless things that she could not have known were true unless she was authentically getting messages from you. I had never met her before and I know that no one in my family ever had. She is friends with the bride's family and I was there as a friend of the groom's family. You also were seen by the man of a completely different ethnicity who painted our house before we moved into it in Arizona. He recounted how, as he was spray painting the garage and both doors were closed, that his tarp moved. When he checked his line to see if it had gotten underneath the tarp, he realized that his line was nowhere near the tarp. He said that he would have likely dismissed the tarp incident but that the day after the painting was finished, and I was in the house cleaning cupboards, he came to do some finishing tasks when someone threw a stone and hit his hand, just before it hit and imprinted the newly painted door in the garage that leads into the house. He ran outside to see if there were any kids playing pranks, but no one was around. As he told me this story, I stared at him in awe and was speechless. He interpreted my reaction to mean that I thought he was lying and he proceeded to tell me that he would not make this story up. I reassured him that I totally believed him, without telling him that I had lost a son and now knew, even before moving in, that you had traveled with us. I could write an entire book about all of the signs including the "Tyler trees" that you drew, painted and stamped on most of your belongings, prior to pictures of trees becoming popular and in every store as drawings, purses, jewelry, etc. When we were in the process of driving to Arizona to relocate and

Seth picked out the hotels each night, as your dad and I drove two separate loaded-down cars, the first hotel he chose, a Holiday Inn Express in St. Louis, had a Tyler tree picture on each and every door as well as a section of Tyler trees in the lobby displayed on the walls and a table. I could go into great detail about how shocked I was to hear the song, "You are My Sunshine" on a Whirlpool commercial about the quality of life, as that was the song I sang to you when you were little, changing the words to personalize it to you. Of course, "You are My Sunshine" trinkets, pictures, artwork, pillows, etc. are everywhere now. A niece by marriage that you only saw once a year on Thanksgiving Day, had a dream with you skateboarding in it. She never knew that you had a skateboard, as she'd never been to our house or seen yours. She looked through all of your Facebook pictures to see if there was a picture of you with your skateboard, but there was not. Again, so many signs . . .

I, prior to your death, never read any books about spiritual life. I didn't know the definition or the role of either a medium or a mystic. I wasn't sure what I believed about life after death, although I always believed in eternal life. I just never thought about what it looked like. Now, I've encountered so many people who have relayed meaningful things about your life after death including a medium and a mystic. I'm reading books about people who have died on the operating table or in a medical crisis, only to return to life and tell about their experiences. Some of these books are written by children who couldn't know how to make up the same information told by countless adults. I'm reading books written by scientists who changed the way they practiced and thought because of paranormal experiences. It was never important for me to think about these issues. Now it is. Now that I've lost you, my twenty-six year old son, it is of paramount importance for me to know where you are, that you are alive, and what life is like for you on the other side. The words on pages from people who have devoted their lives to studying about life after death have such important meaning for me in my life. Almost all of it makes sense and resonates as truth with me even though it's something I know so little about. It's like I have an entirely new room in my brain now, learning and storing critical new information about something so very, very significant and important.

The word "Release." It was planted in my mind the day that I found you. It was never my word. I don't speak that word or write that word, and yet it was there. Just one word in the front of my mind, RELEASE. I've thought about that word thousands of times. RELEASE. What it means. It means so many different things, Tyler. I think that it means that you were released from this physical world, and from all the pain, addiction, and torment that you lived with most days of the last several years of your life. It means that you were released from the guilt you told me that you felt, from the hell that you knew that you put your family through, from the pain of losing relationships including two girls that you loved, as well as some great friends. I believe that it also applies to

Ron, Seth, and me. We are now released from the dark world that you brought, without intent, into our lives. We are released to live a completely different life. We are released from you and your pain, which was our pain too. Although it pains us not to you have you in our lives and in our family, it is a release from a world that we didn't want you to have to live in, and one that we didn't invite, contemplate, or desire. It's a mixed blessing, that RELEASE.

And the writing of this book. I talked to you about my visions of writing books that I started seeing almost ten years ago. I had visions of talking to people about what I'd written. I saw you there with me in all of the visions. After you died, I asked my psychologist about seeing you with me in three consecutive sessions, because I was doubting my visions for the first time. You were gone and yet in my visions you were with me, speaking to others. The doctor finally verbalized that you would still be with me . . . those few words provided extreme comfort and reassurance for me, as I didn't want to consider that those visions were wrong; now I know that they are not. If I can help one addict or the family of one addict, with this book, I know that my life will have purpose. So will your death. There's nothing that I want more.

I love you, Tyler. I always have. I always will.

Love,
Moo

P.S. Sometimes I ask myself, if I had the choice, would I do it all again? Every lie, every stolen dime, every worry and anxiety, the oppressive notion of threats and the dark world, the embarrassment and shame? Would I go through all of that again to have you as my son? Absolutely! In a heartbeat. Without a doubt . . .

NOTE TO READERS

To Anyone,

If you are someone with an addiction, please remember that you are loved. There are people whose lives will never be the same if you die. Hearts will break if you leave this world. Tears will be shed and multiple relationships will be destroyed. Seek help. Find a group. Go to a church. Talk to a counselor or a doctor. Call a friend. Use one of the resources below.

Don't leave your mother/father without their son or daughter. Don't leave friends wondering what else they could or should have done to help you. Don't leave an empty place at the dinner table. Don't leave your name on people's cell phone Favorite list, with no physical person attached to that name anymore. Don't do it. You are worthy of life. You are worthy of love.

Check out one of the following resources. Help IS available. It may seem hard to access, but it's there. You can get better if you want to. You truly can. Remember that you are on this earth for a reason. You may not know what it is, but there is at least one reason. Your life serves a purpose.

RESOURCES

(Note: The author has no personal experience with any
of these but they seem reputable to her. Empathetic
people did answer all of the phone numbers!)

<u>Phone Numbers:</u>

- 888-744-0069-Drug Abuse hotline
- 888-319-2606 Recovery.org
- 800-784-6776-NASAIC (National Alcoholism & Substance Abuse Information Center)
- 844-686-7476 24-Hour GoodDrugs Helpline
- 800-662-HELP-SAMHSA (Substance Abuse & Mental Health Services Administration) National Helpline
- 866-660-6829-InTherooms.org

<u>Websites:</u>

- DrugAbuse.com
- Recovery.org
- hhsgov.opiods
- TheGoodDrugsGuide.com
- InTherooms.org
- Turntohelp.com-helps you find treatment-doctor office, counseling, in-patient, clinic with methadone, 12-step
- www.na.org Narcotics Anonymous (NA)
- www.na.org/meetingsearch-Find a meeting NA (The NA Meeting Search app version 2.0 is now available for your smartphone or tablet)

<u>Texting:</u>

- TEXT "GO" TO 741-741-FREE, 24/7, CONFIDENTIAL.Crisis text line; trained crisis counselors

<u>Social Media:</u>

- InTherooms.org-online social Network for people already in Recovery, Seeking Immediate Help from any Addiction, and their Family, Friends and Allies. Unlimited access to over 117 live online Recovery meetings weekly.

AFTERWORD

The picture on the front cover, Moo believes, depicts the imprisonment that Tyler felt with his addiction. The lock that is on the inside demonstrates that Tyler knew that only he could release himself. This picture is one that Tyler took of himself while in high school.

Note:

A minimum of 10% of all proceeds from the sale of this book will help sponsor someone in need of drug rehabilitation, help fund research to prevent drug addiction, or assist in any related drug prevention/rehabilitation cause.

35620797R00107

Made in the USA
Middletown, DE
09 October 2016